GEORGE BERNARD SHAW

David Ross

GEDDES & GROSSET

ISBN 1 84205 050 8

Printed and bound in Scotland

CONTENTS

'He was a fastidious intellectual, but of course of an Irish type.'
Gilbert Murray

'Of course, as an Irishman, I have some fluency, and can manage a bit of rhetoric and a bit of humour on occasion; and that goes a long way in England.'
George Bernard Shaw, interviewed in The Candid Friend, *1901*

CHAPTER ONE

*T*WO CITIES

London in the 1890s could claim to be the greatest city on earth. Its population was numbered in millions, amounting to easily twice that of the whole of Ireland. It had the world's busiest harbour and was the centre of world trade in just about every essential commodity. The world's first underground railways ran in sulphurous tunnels beneath its overcrowded streets, themselves packed with horse-drawn traffic. From a central high point, like the dome of St Paul's Cathedral, its streets stretched to the horizon in every direction, losing themselves in a smoky brown haze from countless coal-burning chimneys. Within its ever-expanding boundaries, it comprised just about every nationality and every human activity. It was the capital of a rich country, and the centre of a huge colonial empire. The extremes of wealth and poverty, virtue and crime, privilege and exploitation, existed in close proximity to one another. Splendid public buildings of florid architecture reflected this wealth: museums, galleries, also the town palaces of a wealthy aristocracy and of new-moneyed industrial millionaires. At its core, in one or two exclusive districts, lived a social hierarchy, each of its grades carefully codified and kept in records, like Burke's *Peerage*, that formed a social stud-book. At the very peak of this structure was the monarch, Victoria, the aged and reclusive Queen-Empress, now so old that she had outlived her former unpopularity and was more of a totem than a person to most of her subjects. In orderly ranks below her were royal dukes, non-royal dukes, earls, viscounts, barons, baronets, knights, and the broad range of 'the gentry', who possessed no titles but who owned land and shares, had money in the banks, employed servants, kept carriages of their own, and considered themselves to be very much part of the fabric of social life. From their ranks came the army officers, the vicars and parsons of the Church of England, the professors at the universities, the lawyers, the doctors. At the upper end of their own scale, they had titled relatives; at the lower end, they had connections with the mercantile classes, tradesmen, small farmers, artisans. 'society' from the gentry up consisted of less than two per cent of the population.

The other ninety-eight per cent of the inhabitants of London, and of England, had no position in 'Society'. They were the workers of the colossal hive. However, there was no equality of status among them. The reflection of a hierarchical society went all the way through the population. At its lowest end were the newly arrived and the disadvantaged: immigrants, beggars, single mothers, the old, the ill, the unlucky, the unskilled, the unambitious, the exploited. By far the largest group of all was the 'working classes' – whose name defined their function. They were the machine-minders, the stokers of furnaces, the sempstresses, domestic servants, railwaymen, road-menders, house-builders, stable-boys, waitresses, artisans of all sorts, with their own gradations of status from apprentice to journeyman to foreman; from skivvy to parlour-maid to cook-housekeeper, boot-boy to footman to butler. They merged into a middle class of people, the structure of which is harder to define.

In this group, wives did not normally work. Unmarried women frequently did, and had to to survive, but the work they did was of a genteel nature: decorative embroidery rather than operating a machine to sew mass-produced shirts. Governesses were still in demand for the children of the well-off. The word 'typewriter' originally referred to the woman who typed at the machine, not the machine itself. The still-recent legislation enforcing universal education was a godsend to a generation of intelligent women who were recruited as elementary school teachers. The middle class was a fluid one. Entrance to it could be achieved in different ways: by having money, by working to gain a qualification, by marriage. The pace of technological change and development meant a steady demand for engineers, laboratory assistants, draughtsmen, trained nurses, clerks and clerkesses, salespeople. Managers became more necessary as businesses grew larger and more complex. All these might consider themselves as members of the middle class. The key to being part of it was having at least one domestic servant in the house. Labour at the bottom end of the scale, especially female labour, was cheap.

The border between middle class and gentry was becoming blurred. In the new science of sociology, the term 'upper-middle-class' would be required, to apply to those whose status was 'gentry' but who had arrived through professional eminence (or the professional eminence of a parent) rather than through inheriting land. There was a strong current of upward mobility, with real opportunity for ability and enterprise to display itself.

But despite the current of social advancement, there were also huge constraints. Opportunities were limited. There was a strong urge, on the part of those in the more comfortable and privileged sections of society, to keep the rest in their place. But the working class had an important asset. By political processes deplored by many in the upper classes, they possessed power, or at least the men did. Men over twenty-one could vote. Universal suffrage was still more than thirty years away, but the working class, with its vast proportion of the population, was, as a number of clever people had already realised, some to their alarm, others to their satisfaction, capable of electing or dismissing the Imperial Government.

Karl Marx, who had died in 1883, had lived the last thirty-four years of his life in London. In the Reading Room of the British Museum he researched and wrote his book, *Capital*, which would be a basic text for the Communist revolution in Russia. Marx's view, conditioned by his seeing a huge industrial 'proletariat' in Germany and Britain – regimented, hard-worked, poorly paid, creating wealth whose fruits were enjoyed only by a few – was that the working class would rise against its oppressors, capitalism would be replaced by socialism, and the power of the state would wither away in an ultimately classless society. The English working class however refused to behave acording to Marx's own prediction. As he was to acknowledge, there was no real revolutionary spirit in the country. Something in the fibre or mental make-up of the English resisted the call. Marx admitted with some bafflement: 'The English have all the materials required for a revolution. What they lack is the spirit of generalisation and revolutionary ardour.' Among the English there was a strong sense of conservatism. They had seen enormous social change over three generations and could sense that there was more to come. But they preferred gradual and invisible revolutions to grand lurches. The stability of social institutions was valued, and even most reformers argued for development rather than for root-and-branch changes. The English tended towards practical action rather than idealistic fervour. Theirs was a materialist society. Whilst in Germany philosophical ideas were being advanced in a climate of idealism and speculation, the English instinct was largely hostile to such thought, and English thinkers of the time preferred to stick to what was known or could be objectively established. This practical application, and the science of comparison, analysis and deduction had resulted in Great Britain producing two scientific movements as revolutionary in their own way as Marxism – the science of geology had been established in Scotland and proceeded to destroy the long-held Biblical theory of Creation; and Charles Darwin's theory of natural selection had both compounded this and also radically altered the human race's view of where it stood in relation to the universe – a group of beings not created by God in his own image but descended through many generations from apes. These theories had provoked arguments and counter-theories which still rolled and reverberated through intellectual discussion, whether at the Piccadilly rooms of the Royal Society or the Mechanics' Institute of any town.

In the bustling metropolis there were of course many people who did not fit conformably into the nice gradations of London social life. There were mercurial elements which did not adjust themselves tidily to expectation. They were creative spirits.

In the London of the 1890s, among the seven million or so inhabitants, were many who had been born in Ireland or who were of Irish parentage. The vast majority of this Irish population came from the country peasantry whose parents or grandparents had been forced out by poverty, hunger, the rent-demands of absentee landlords, and acute awareness of an almost total lack of any opportunity to improve their hand-to-mouth existence. Ireland was still part of the 'United Kingdom', as it had been since its Parliament was incorporated into the Westminster Parliament in 1800. The Irish shared British citizenship with English, Scots and Welsh. Almost all of this Irish immigrant population of London was included in the working classes, and almost all of it retained the Roman Catholic religion of its ancestors. There were other sorts of Irish, however. Ireland itself was a country whose history had left it with three incompatible elements in its population. By far the greatest was the Catholic population of the rural districts (often still Gaelic-speaking) and the towns and cities. In some of the northern counties, however, the bulk of the population, though also of Celtic stock, was Protestant, and there had been a long history of mutual hostility between the religious groups. In all the larger towns, especially Dublin, there were Protestant trades-men and merchants. Though these were often of English or Scottish ancestry, they had been established in Ireland for generations, and often had no family connections on the other side of the Irish Sea; Ireland was their only home. But the bond of language and religion, together with a political need to maintain the Union with England, meant that England was not to them an alien place, though it might be an unknown one. The third and smallest element in the population was the aristocracy and landed gentry. These were the 'Anglo-Irish' and they moved with ease between the two countries. The wealthiest had estates and houses in both. Some of them sat in the House of Lords. The social divisions of Ireland, inten-sified by religion, language, heritage and genealogy, were more rigid than those of England. Ireland's lack of industrial development had inhibited the growth of a substantial mid-dle class like the one which had arisen in England.

In the previous decade, it had seemed certain that Ireland was about to see restoration of 'Home Rule', with the re-establishment of a Parliament in Dublin. This was welcome to many of the Protestant community, and indeed its mem-bers had been prominent both in the armed struggle for Irish independence of the eighteenth century and the politi-cal struggle of the later nineteenth. Most notable had been Charles Stewart Parnell, who had led the Irish Parliamentar-ians through the 1880s and whose political strategy seemed destined to be highly successful until it was wrecked in 1890 by his involvement in a divorce suit. He died in 1891. Parnell's death and the following disunity among Irish MPs brought an end to any near likelihood of an Irish Parliament,

17

whether it was for limited home rule or total independence. Nationalists now concentrated on promoting things Irish: Irish culture, Irish games and the Irish language. There was a sense that the people needed to be reminded and convinced of their Irishness before the political struggle could be effectively resumed.

Meanwhile, for an ambitious young Irishman, it was plain that the opportunities offered by London were wider and greater than those available in Dublin. Especially so for an ambitious young Protestant Irishman.

Among the many Irish in London in the early 1890s were three of especial interest. They were all Dublin-born writers, creative figures and so members of that 'mercurial' group which slid most readily through the gradations of society. None of them was a member of the top bracket of the Anglo-Irish gentry. The nearest to this pinnacle was Oscar Wilde, born in 1854 and now in his forties. His father had been a Dublin doctor at the top of his profession, knighted as Sir William Wilde. Wilde was known as a poet and aesthete, and a writer of fairy tales and stories. His career as a playwright was just about to burst into great success with 'Lady Windermere's Fan' in 1892. The youngest of the three was William Butler Yeats, born in 1865. He had spent much of his boyhood in London, where his father had been trying to establish himself as a portrait-painter. Since 1887 he had been back in London, living with his family, working to establish himself as a poet, existing in a condition of genteel poverty. The third was George Bernard Shaw. He had been born in Dublin in 1856 and lived in London since 1876, in a social and financial state very like that of Yeats for much of the time.

By the early 1890s he was known as a brilliant journalist whose range went from social and political issues to music and drama criticism. He had written five completely unsuccessful novels and his first play had ended after two performances.

By the end of the decade all three would be famous. Wilde indeed would end it as notorious, following his prosecution for immorality, but his dazzling comedies went on being performed, with the author's name pasted over on the handbills. He died in Paris in 1900. Yeats's fame was more limited but his reputation as a poet was steadily rising. Shaw had emerged as London's leading modern dramatist. All three knew each other. Wilde had been kind to the impoverished young William Yeats. Yeats and Shaw had a common connection through the household of William Morris, the wealthy poet, arts organiser, and pioneer socialist, who had befriended both.

Of the three, Yeats was most involved with their home country. Part of his vision was to establish a modern Irish literature, written in English, and Ireland continued to be a prime source of his inspiration, even though he spent almost as much time in England as he did there. Wilde was not concerned with Ireland. Shaw never forgot that he was an Irishman, and like Yeats was a Unionist who believed in Home Rule. But, though much in his thought and writing is Irish, he did not feel the rootedness in Irish history and culture that Yeats felt and nourished. He wanted to reform not Ireland or even England, but the world. His career and that of the younger poet, with many fascinating parallels, form an intriguing counterpoint through the decades between 1890 and 1939, when Yeats died.

They were not the only Irish literary men on the London scene. George Moore was there too, in 1890 a more considerable figure than the other three, but history has left Wilde, Yeats and Shaw acknowledged as men of genius, whilst relegating Moore to a lower order. His novels have a sentence or two in literary histories. Shaw, Yeats and Wilde as well as being men of genius, were men of magnanimity. They could fight, and scheme, and indulge in enmities, but their enmities were rarely petty, and their attitudes were rarely mean ones. This can not be said of George Moore.

Looking back on these three men of 1890, more than a century later, the reasons for their continued fame can be discerned. Wilde, who though he said he had put his genius into his life and his talent into his works, has yet to be surpassed as a master of comic wit on the stage. Yeats's poetry, for many, comes closest to catching the troubled underlying spirit of the twentieth century. Shaw, who outlived Wilde by half a century and Yeats by eleven years, revolutionized English drama, but his main contribution was in helping to create a change in the whole climate of ideas. Though England did not know it, he was out to shake up that encrusted social structure, to blow raspberries at its tendency to imperial self-satisfaction, to challenge its comfortable materialism and distaste for 'ideas', and to question some of its most cherished attitudes. In a word, he wanted to teach it how to be a modern society.

CHAPTER II

A DUBLIN BOY

The youngest of three children, and the only boy, George Bernard Shaw was born on July 26, 1856, at 3, Upper Synge Street, Dublin (now 33 Synge Street). His father, George Carr Shaw, and his mother, Lucinda Elizabeth Gurly, were an ill-assorted couple. His father's background was the Protestant mercantile class. Two of his relatives were Church of Ireland parsons, but the most socially eminent was Sir Robert Shaw, a baronet and son of the founder of the Royal Bank of Ireland. The name Bernard came from George Carr Shaw's father, who was a lawyer and became High Sheriff of Kilkenny. This Bernard Shaw collapsed and died when George was twelve years old, as a result of his business partner's running off with all the money in the business. George, the eighth of fifteen children, was brought up by his mother. Despite his father's ruin and death, he had hopes that others among his well-placed male relations would provide him with the kind of undemanding but well-paid employment that was still available, to those with the right connections, in the 1830s. He grew up to be a good-natured, ineffective individual. Through his uncle, Sir Robert, he got a sinecure in the Law Courts, but such 'jobs' were vanishing; there were protests, and in 1850 they were abolished. George Carr Shaw received instead an official pension of £50 a year, which he commuted for a lump sum of £500. This he invested in a milling business, along with a friend who was in the cloth trade. The business was never a great success; his partner soon withdrew, but it staggered along, enabling George Shaw to live modestly well on it, and to indulge an increasing fondness for the bottle.

He was thirty-seven when he married Lucinda. The Gurlys saw themselves as socially a step up from the Shaws, since they were landed proprietors in County Carlow. Lucinda's father was, however, a financially irresponsible figure who was constantly in debt, almost a caricature of the feckless and improvident landlord. Lucinda's son was to describe her education in these terms:

'Though she had been severely educated up to the highest standard for Irish "carriage ladies" of her time, she was much more like a Trobriand Islander ... than like a modern Cambridge lady graduate in respect of accepting all the habits, good or bad, of the Irish society in which she was brought up as part of an uncontrollable order of nature ... She knew nothing of the value of money nor of housekeeping nor of hygiene nor of anything that could be left to servants or governesses or parents or solicitors or apothecaries or any other member of the retinue, indoor and outdoor, of a country house.'

She was sent to Dublin to live with a ferocious aunt, and made the social acquaintance of George Carr Shaw. They became engaged, an engagement which the aunt was opposed to, telling Lucinda that Shaw was well known as a drinker. When she taxed him with this, George denied it and told her that he was a teetotaller, which indeed he was – in principle. He was a secret, solitary and ashamed drinker. Lucinda accepted his word on this, and was never to forgive him for the lie.

The marriage of George Bernard Shaw's parents thus got off to a troubled start. Lucinda was cut out out of her aunt's will (the old lady was to leave £4000, no small amount for these days). On their honeymoon, spent in a hotel in Liverpool, Lucinda discovered a cache of George's bottles in a cupboard, and ran away, but with nowhere to go in a strange city, had to come back to some kind of reconciliation. In the course of the next four years the three children were born.

It was not a happy home. Lucinda had very little money; George had only the sporadic income of the ill-run corn business with which to maintain his family and his habit. Families can be happy in genteel poverty, but the Shaw family was not such a one. The father continued his drinking and continued to be ashamed of it. Quiet and undemonstrative when sober, he became less inhibited when drunk. His suppressed emotions came out in anger and shouting. Once, out on a walk with his young son, he playfully threatened to throw him into the Grand Canal and pretended he was actually going to do it. On returning home, the boy said to his mother: 'Mamma, I think Papa is drunk,' to which she replied: 'When is he anything else?' The young George Bernard, known to the family as 'Sonny', vividly remembered the scorn with which she said it, and his own surprise.

His own rigid abstinence from alcohol has been put down to his distaste and shame at his father's drinking. This may be correct, but Shaw also became a convinced vegetarian, and it has not been suggested that this was because of his mother's cooking. Coming from such a background, he could easily develop his own obsessions and oddities. There was a strong temperance movement in Dublin and in Ireland generally, begun earlier in the nineteenth century by Father Mathew, a Catholic priest, and supported by all denominations. But St John Ervine, one of Shaw's biographers, and a long-time friend, recorded that: 'His memory of his father's tippling was long and deep, and it made him a lifelong teetotaller.' George Carr Shaw, as a father, was a bad role-model and gave his children little attention or support. Yet there were moments when father and son achieved some closeness, and George clearly performed some of the rites required of a father:

'When I was a child he gave me my first dip in the sea in Killiney Bay. He prefaced it by a very serious exhortation on the importance of learning to swim, culminating in these words, "When I was a boy of only fourteen, my knowledge of swimming enabled me to save your uncle Robert's life." Then seeing that I was deeply impressed, he stooped, and added confidentially in my ear, "and, to tell you the truth, I was never so sorry for anything in my life afterwards." He then plunged into the ocean, enjoyed a thoroughly refreshing swim and chuckled all the way home.'

George Carr Shaw has had a bad press, led by his son, and

followed by his son's biographers, and probably deserved it. But in that silent-when-sober man, dismissed often as 'little' and 'ineffectual', there was something powerful but frustrated, which never saw the light of day in its own right. He had deceived his wife about his drinking, but Lucinda had little or no affection for him, nor any feeling for him other than disdain. He was caught in a loveless marriage, with children who were repelled by his boozing, and took their cue from their mother's coldness to him, but he did not desert it or them. About the time his son was fourteen, and after decades of heavy drinking, he collapsed one day on his own doorstep. Warned by his doctor that further drinking would kill him, he stopped. Many ineffectual men have been unable to hold to such a decision, but George Carr Shaw stuck to it. There was a strong will beneath the easy-going outward impression that he gave.

Lucinda Shaw showed little affection to her children. She was not unkind or cruel, but merely unloving. Young Shaw grew up in a home where there there was no love or tenderness. A physical resemblance to his father may have contributed to his mother's attitude: her own father was a rapscallion, her husband a drunk – what chance was there for the son? In some such cases, a servant or nurse provides what the mother lacks, but the Shaw children do not appear to have derived much from the succession of ill-paid servants employed by their parents:

'We children were abandoned entirely to servants who … were utterly unfit to be trusted with the charge of three cats, much less three children. I had my meals in the kitchen,

mostly of stewed beef, which I loathed, badly cooked pota-
toes, sound or diseased as the case might be, much too much
tea of brown delft teapots left to "draw" on the hob until it
was pure tannin.'

Shaw wrote this in the preface to *London Music*, of 1888–
89, and more than fifty years after that, his bitterness about
his childhood had not died down: 'The way we were
brought up, or rather not brought up, doesn't bear thinking
of', he wrote to his friend Ada Tyrrell in 1942. Dressed and
fed by people who cared nothing for him, he was a sufferer
from emotional neglect. The more he tried to make an impression on his mother, the more she rebuffed him. Nor, it
seems, did the three children band together to give one another support and comfort. The boy was effectively on his
own: 'I was taken, and took myself for, a disagreeable little
beast. Nobody concerned himself or herself as to what I was
capable of becoming, nor did I', he wrote to Mrs Patrick
Campbell. This was not strictly true. Both the Shaw parents
were conscious of their social position. The children were
reminded of this. When the boy Sonny talked or played to
the children of the lower orders, his father told him off. On
one such occasion the other child was the son of an iron-
monger, a retail shopkeeper almost certainly wealthier than
George Carr Shaw. But Mr Shaw was the proprietor of a
milling business, and the relation of a baronet – he did not
consider it proper for his son to mix with the offspring of
tradesmen.

The parents went through the motions of doing the right
thing. A teacher was hired to come to the house and give the
two girls and their brother an elementary education. Shaw

learned to read and write, to add and subtract. At a tender age, he was writing letters for the illiterate servants, to their dictation. The only thing that moved his parents was music. There was a piano in the house, and a neighbour recalled the child: 'He wore a holland tunic and went by the name of Sonny. He was always rather apart from the others and would be seen sitting at the piano, picking out airs with one finger or absorbed in the construction of a toy theatre.' Music was of course the chief diversion of most middle-class homes in the Victorian era, when entertainment had to be made rather than passively received on a screen, but Shaw's mother, particularly, had a good deal more than the conventional interest in music and song. She was an excellent singer, and had got to know an enterprising professional musician, George John Vandeleur Lee, who was a singing teacher and also the leader of an orchestra. Voice production was Lee's speciality, and he had a theory of his own about how best the singer could develop and project the voice. Mrs Shaw was a keen pupil, and the Vandeleur system, known as 'The Method', certainly helped her. Later in life it would help her son, although he was no singer, to be a most effective public speaker, able to control and manage his voice in a way that few orators could achieve. The Shaws held musical evenings for friends, under the direction of Vandeleur Lee. Music was something that could bridge the gaps between sections of society. The withdrawn boy was sharply observant and noted that:

'My first doubt as to whether God could really be a good Protestant was suggested by the fact that the best voices available for the combination with my mother's in the works of the great composers had been unaccountably vouchsafed to Roman Catholics. Even the Divine Gentility was presently called in question, for some of these vocalists were undeniably shopkeepers. If the best tenor, undeniably a Catholic, was at least an accountant, the buffo was a frank stationer. There was no help for it: if my mother was to do anything but sing silly ballads in drawing rooms, she had to associate herself on an entirely unsectarian footing with people of like artistic gifts without the smallest reference to creed or class. She must actually permit herself to be approached by Roman Catholic priests, and at their invitation to enter that house of Belial, the Roman Catholic Chapel, and sing the Masses of Mozart there.'

Mrs Shaw in fact was a self-avowed atheist at this time, but of course a Protestant atheist. She did a lot of work for Vandeleur Lee, transcribing music, writing out parts, and assisting him in the production of amateur operas. She is also believed to have composed songs in her own right. Lee, whose role in the household must often have seemed a more imposing one than George Carr Shaw's, was to play a very important part in the Shaw family life. A bachelor, who had lived with an invalid brother until the brother's death, he made a remarkable proposal to the Shaws in 1866. This was that they should move from Synge Street and share with him a large house he had bought in Hatch Street, not far away but definitely smarter. He had also bought a cottage at Dalkey, which the Shaws were free to use.

The offer was accepted. The household acquired a further occasional resident in Shaw's uncle Walter, his mother's brother, a ship's doctor, who used it as his home base between voyages. Walter took after his father, the country squire, and was a man of free talk, no beliefs, and a rude sense of humour. He seems to have got on with George Carr Shaw better than his sister did. When Walter was around there was plenty of talk, of a kind to which Sonny listened avidly. At school, and at the Sunday School to which he was sent, the boy was being taught a great deal of Scriptural knowledge, much of which was subverted by the conversation in Hatch Street, where the three men would discuss such matters as how the miracles of Christ could have been rigged. Shaw later recorded how his father told him that: '... even the worst enemy of religion could say no worse of the Bible than that it was the damnedest parcel of lies ever written. He would then rub his eyes and chuckle for quite a long time.'

Such scepticism, irreverence, and verbal wit were not to be lost on the young Shaw.

At some point in his young boyhood, Sonny was taken by his mother to visit the aunt who had warned her against marrying Carr Shaw. If it was hoped that this would mollify the old lady, it was in vain. From another relative on his father's side, the Rev George Carroll, he was given Latin lessons, and may also have imbibed some sense of a more nationalist and radical political outlook than his father possessed, as Carroll, unusually for a Church of Ireland clergyman, was a nationalist. At the age of eleven George Bernard was sent to school at the Wesleyan Connexional School. He was later to refer to himself as a dunce but in fact he appears to have been both lively and clever when a subject took his interest. Nevertheless, he did not remain there long. At Vandeleur Lee's suggestion, his parents transferred him to the Central Model School. Officially this school was non-sectarian, which may have had some appeal to his parents, as well as to the irreligious Lee. In fact, however, the majority of the pupils there were Roman Catholic.

Sonny Shaw had been taught for a long time of the significance of his social position. His parents, though they did not mix at all in the grander social world that existed round Dublin Castle, where the Lord Lieutenant of Ireland had his headquarters, still considered themselves to be part of the elite, the 'Protestant Ascendancy', and had a correspondingly poor view of Catholics. Now they were sending their son to a school which was in effect a school for Catholic boys. To him, at the impressionable age of twelve, it was a source of deep shame. It seemed to proclaim to the world how little his parents thought or cared about him. He loathed his time there, which lasted about seven months. Eventually he refused to return, and was sent instead to the portentously named Dublin English Scientific and Commercial Day School, based in a handsome old town house at the corner of Aungier Street and Whitefriar Street; an efficient place which, as its name suggests, was English and Protestant in its outlook. Here he settled down and became a model pupil. He also began to make friends, including Matthew McNulty, who became a close friend and who wrote an account of their schooldays and later experiences.

Young Shaw did not like Mr Vandeleur Lee, who was responsible for sending him to the Central Model School, who monopolised his mother's interest and who was now taking a close interest in his elder sister Lucy, now seventeen. Lucy too had a fine voice, which Lee was training, but Lee, not a man of physical charm, had fallen in love with her. Lucy did not respond to his advances. Sonny could not sing and so was of no particular interest to the master of 'The Method', but the boy became fascinated by music. Listening to endless exercises and rehearsals, as a child he became familiar with much of the musical repertoire of the time, later noting of such operas as 'Il Trovatore', 'Don Giovanni', 'Faust' and 'Lucrezia Borgia': 'I whistled and sang them from the first bar to the last whilst I was a small boy.' Music was to be very important to him. In the composition of his plays and especially their frequent long speeches, opera was very much in his mind, and he often made a direct comparison between his speeches and operatic arias.

Lee's invitation to the Shaw family to use his Dalkey seaside house, Torca Cottage, was also welcome to the boy. Born and brought up in the city, he was very much a town child. There were no visits to country relatives, like the young Yeats's holidays in Sligo, to give him a greater sense of Ireland and its indigenous culture. But Torca Cottage, with its views of the Wicklow Hills and its openness to the sea and the sky, was a place of delight for him.

Other interests he appears to have discovered for himself. It was not a bookish household; Mr Shaw was not interested in literature, and Mrs Shaw was only interested in music, but he had some access to books, and read widely but without particular discrimination, perhaps depending on what was available. He read Dickens with great enjoyment; the great novelist was still writing in 1866, though he had written all

31

his novels except for the posthumous and unfinished *Edwin Drood;* and they had all the immediacy and freshness of great works in their own time. In the Wesleyan school, Sonny was already making up stories using the name of a Dickensian character, Lobjoit, as his hero. He also became interested in fine art and whilst still a teenager had spent enough time in the National Gallery to recognise the works and style of individual painters.

The family life, though unusual, might have seemed to have become stable. Lee however was ambitious for himself and 'The Method'. In 1869 he published a book on his system, which was well-received in Dublin and came out in a second edition in London: *The Voice: Its Artistic Production, Development and Preservation.* Encouraged by this, Lee resolved to leave Dublin for London, where the potential pupils were not only far more numerous, but also richer, and where there was a far more active musical life. This was dismaying news to the female Shaws, or at least to Lucinda. It meant the end of Torca Cottage and of Hatch Street, which they could not keep up on their own. Lee however, had his own career and fame to consider, and though he did not leave Dublin until 1872, the Shaws were incapable of making any satisfactory arrangements for themselves.

One decision was made – Sonny would have to leave school. His father could not afford to keep him there; rather it was necessary that he should contribute to the family by bringing in a salary. His sisters were not employable: Lucy was still immersed in her singing lessons; Agnes was already suffering from the tuberculosis that would kill her. In 1871, George's brother Richard, who worked in the Irish Valuation Office, arranged for his nephew to become a clerk in the office of an estate agency, Uniacke and Townshend. That was the end of Shaw's formal education. He had entertained thoughts of becoming an opera singer or an artist. Reality found him at 15, Molesworth Street, in the city centre, writing entries in ledgers, and earning eighteen shillings a week. This again hardly seems like what might have been expected by a boy brought up to consider himself part of the country's elite social group. The normal progression for a clever boy of the ascendancy would be to Trinity College, followed by a professional post in the law or the Church or government service. To become a junior clerk in an office seemed to point to a very different status.

But it was not as bad as it might seem, and Shaw did not undergo the desperate sense of mortification that the Central Model School had inflicted upon him. Estate agents had a certain social position. They dealt with and on behalf of property owners, and property meant gentility. And Uniacke Townshend was a high-class agency, whose clients included members of the gentry. Some of Shaw's young colleagues were 'premium apprentices', who had already graduated from Trinity and whose fathers had paid for them to be there and get some business grounding in property management. Hesketh Pearson, in his biography of Shaw, describes the atmosphere there as 'intensely snobbish'. Even a junior clerk in the business could feel that he was still part of the Ascendancy, and indeed be quite involved, part of the 'Who's up, who's down?' and 'Who's selling to whom?' gossip network that is generated in such a business and such a society.

Shaw found his work easily within his powers. The agency

recognised his ability and he was swiftly promoted. His relative youth and humble salaried status did not prevent him from becoming friendly with the premium apprentices, and he enjoyed argument and discussion with them. Even when his relative ignorance was pointed out, as on one occasion when a better-educated colleague said: 'What is the use of arguing when you don't know what a syllogism is?' he was not daunted in defeat, but set out to learn something about logic. The irrepressible and jaunty public self-confidence that was to characterise Shaw as an adult was already beginning to display itself in the adolescent. By the time he was sixteen, Shaw's superior, the chief cashier, was sacked for helping himself to the firm's money; the teenager was given his job, first on a temporary, then a permanent basis. His salary was increased to £48 a year. As chief cashier he did not simply sit behind a desk. He went out to collect rents due for collection, often from slum properties, travelled into the countryside to visit estates managed by the agency, learned how to administer a whole range of detail relating to banking procedures, property insurance, land registry and the legalities of property sales; and knew a great deal of his employers' confidential business.

If his ambition had not extended beyond a respectable salaried post, he might have remained at Uniacke Townshend for the rest of his life, still as a manager, since his lack of capital made it impossible for him to aspire to a partnership or to start his own business. But he already had other intentions, though they seemed far from likely to come to anything.

During his first year at the agency, the family's home life finally collapsed. Vandeleur Lee left for England. Mrs

Shaw very soon followed him, with her daughters. George Carr Shaw and his son remained in Dublin. Mrs Shaw sent the girls to Ventnor, in the Isle of Wight, where the climate was supposed to be favourable to consumptives. She bought a house in Victoria Grove, off the Fulham Road, in West London. In the course of the rest of her life, she only saw her husband for a week, when he paid her a short visit in London, but there was no divorce or formal separation. She did not return to Dublin, and did not see her son for five years. George Carr Shaw and Sonny moved to lodgings at 61, Harcourt Street. The deserted husband felt no rancour towards his wife. She had taken with her the proceeds of the sale of their furniture, properly speaking his; but he arranged to pay her £52 a year, and did so regularly until his death. For several years their marriage had been a front, with Vandeleur Lee the man in her life. Her final departure was a relief to him, and he maintained a low-key but apparently contented life in Dublin, visiting his friends, reading the newspapers, free from domestic strife. There has been much speculation that Lucinda was Lee's mistress. Shaw himself, though he delivered himself of much bile on the subject of both parents, could never bring himself to believe that of his mother, though his belief was based on character rather than any other evidence. Writing to Frank Harris, he said that a man who could have seduced his mother: 'could have seduced the wooden Virgin at Nuremburg. My mother could have boarded and lodged the three musketeers and D'Artagnan for twenty years without discovering their sex; and they would no more

35

have obtruded it on her than they would have ventured to smoke in her drawing room.'

Like so many utterances of Shaw's, this is delivered with such conviction and gusto, and such entertainment, that it invites assent. He was convinced that his mother was a completely frigid woman. During his early teens, and later on in London, he had ample opportunity to observe the relationship between his mother and Lee, but a sexual relationship would necessarily have been covert. It is entirely likely that Lucinda Shaw followed Lee to London (and settled herself independently there) not out of passion, but out of desperation. Music was the centre of her life; he was intimately associated with that. He was her closest friend and her marriage was a nullity. Also Lucy, her eldest daughter, had ambitions as a singer which were much more likely to be realised in London than in Dublin. Cold as she was, there was a certain bravery in Lucinda Shaw's decision to flout convention and test her fortunes in a huge, unknown city.

The Harcourt Street lodgings of father and son were agreeable to both. Shaw made a valuable new friend there in Dr Chichester Bell, a relative of the inventor of the telephone. Bell was an intellectual whose interest went beyond medicine into physics, chemistry, languages and music. It was he who introduced Shaw properly to the work of Wagner, which previously the youth had despised: 'When I found that Bell regarded Wagner as a great composer, I bought a vocal score of Lohengrin: the only sample to be had at the Dublin music shops. The first few bars completely converted me.'

Matthew McNulty, who had left school at the same time

as Shaw, had become a clerk in the Bank of Ireland. He had literary aspirations, articulated more strongly than Shaw's yet were. Sent to work in Newry, County Down, he found his spare time hanging heavily on his hands, and they exchanged many letters in a high-flown youthful style, each of them harbouring ambitions beyond what their prosaic workaday situations offered. Shaw travelled up to Newry to spend his first independent holiday with McNulty, when he was seventeen. The photograph they had taken of themselves together is the earliest known one of Shaw. Contrary to the practice of most Victorian parents, George and Lucinda either never posed with their children for a family group portrait, or any such thing has long been lost. In the evenings the young men worked together on *The Newry Nights' Entertainment,* a work which has not survived. It was a short period of highly intense emotion, during which the two drew up a declaration of eternal friendship, with numerous pledges attached, including the sharing of each others' prosperity or adversity, the exchange of all their thoughts with total frankness, and that the first to die would appear in spirit to the other. The declaration was signed in blood.

In Dublin, Shaw had few friends. His amiable arguments with the premium apprentices did not lead to invitations to their houses or to meet their sisters. Until McNulty returned from Newry in 1874, he had quite a lonely time of it. George Shaw had no urge to an active social life. The lodging-house did not give Shaw the sort of home base where he could entertain. Still, his relative passivity is surprising, in a city which offered art and music societies to anyone with an interest in these things. Many other things were going on in Dublin in the 1870s, including a heightening of the political climate with the advent of Parnell. (Shaw met Parnell around this time in connection with the estate agency business, and was not impressed, partly perhaps because Parnell and the agency were in dispute and Shaw was always loyal to his own side). Perhaps the departure of his mother had made a more serious impact than he understood, then or later. Teenagers are apt to take things personally. Lucinda's departure from Dublin, for her son, meant a physical abandonment that set the seal on her emotional ignoring of him and told him that, in her eyes, he was worthless. He was left wildly unsure of himself. In a letter to Mrs Patrick Campbell in 1912 he recalls that 'Once in my calfish teens, I fell wildly in love with a lady of your complexion; and she, good woman, having a sister to provide for, set to work to marry me to the sister. Whereupon I shot back into the skies from which I had descended ...' This may have some connection with a cryptic entry in his otherwise mundane diary of these years, referred to as 'The L ... Episode', with the note 'But they laugh best who laugh last'. His jaunty self-confidence went into abeyance and he became increasingly introspective. Long and solitary walks were one form of recreation, but he also began to go to the theatre. He saw Henry Irving at the Gaiety Theatre, and like Yeats a few years later, was immensely impressed, though he did not, like Yeats, set out to imitate the great actor's 'Hamlet walk'. McNulty had developed a strong interest in music, and on his return began to study at the Royal Irish Academy of Music. Shaw applied himself to learning to play the piano. They still talked about their ambitions. Shaw had given up any thought of becoming a painter, and now shared with McNulty the notion of being a writer.

His first published work was a letter to the press, which appeared in *Public Opinion,* on April 3, 1875. It was prompted by the appearance in Dublin of the celebrated American evangelists, Sankey and Moody, whose mass meetings, with their atmosphere whipped up by powerful hymns, confessions of past wrongs, and fervent invitations to come and be 'saved', attracted huge crowds. It is a curious letter, written in response to an earlier one, and mildly deprecates the activity of the evangelists, pointing out its effect on their converts:

'... it has a tendency to make them highly objectionable members of society and introduces their unconverted friends to desire a speedy reaction, which either soon takes place, or the revived one relapses slowly into his previous benighted condition ...'

The letter, signed only 'S.' was shown by Shaw to his colleagues at Uniacke Townshend, creating such a noisy argument that Mr Townshend reprimanded him. Shaw was already feeling restive. He had formed the view that a business like the land agency was there for 'enriching an individual at the expense of the community' (as he wrote to a Dublin contact in 1879) and this offended his sense of what was socially right and responsible. Also, a nephew of Townshend's, without experience, had been put into the office over Shaw's head. Shaw, who talked in his spare time to McNulty about becoming a literary genius, decided it was time to put his aspirations to the test. He resigned from the agency, with a letter which is far more prophetic of the Shaw to come than his mild effusion about the evangelists:

'Dear Sir – I beg to give you notice that at the end of this month I shall leave your office. My reason is that I object to receive a salary for which I give no adequate value. Not having enough to do, it follows that the little I have done is not well done: when I ceased to act as Cashier I anticipated this, and have since become satisfied that I was right. Under these circumstances I prefer to discontinue my services, and remain,

Very truly yours, G. B. Shaw'

Townshend's response was to offer him a salary increase, but Shaw's mind was made up.

On the day on which he left the estate agency, March 31, 1876, his sister Agnes died of tuberculosis at Ventnor.

CHAPTER

III

AN UNWELCOME SON

His resignation from the agency did not mean that Shaw had a firm purpose in view. He had considered a career as a musician, but a short course on the cornet discouraged him. Townshend's increased salary offer may have been inspired by the fear that he would join a rival agency, but Shaw had no intention of pursuing a career in which his best hope was to be a functionary who would never reach the top of the business. And in any case he had come to despise the whole ethos of such a business. The example of his mother, now established as a music teacher in London, had been before him for a few years, and he decided to emulate her, and try his fortune there. He had few regrets at his quitting his native city. In the preface to his novel *Immaturity*, he wrote:

'. . . when I left Dublin I left (a few private friendships apart) no society that did not disgust me. To this day my sentimental regard for Ireland does not include its capital. I am not enamoured of failure, of poverty, of obscurity, and of the ostracism and contempt which these imply; and these were all that Dublin offered to the enormity of my unconscious ambition.'

This was somewhat unfair on Dublin, to which he had offered nothing more of his great ambition than a rather ordinary letter to a magazine. But the sentence is expressive of his inner feelings: if this was how he felt in Dublin, and London was available, it was best to make for there.

With the savings he had made from his salary, he arrived in London richer than he was to be again for several years. He went to his mother's house, where he was received with no great show of affection after their five-year separation. But she did not turn him out. Early on, he travelled with his sister Lucy to the Isle of Wight to visit Agnes's grave, then returned to live with her and his mother. Mrs Shaw was making her living by teaching music. Lucy was working on her voice and her ambition to be a great opera singer. The young man, arrived from Dublin with the hope of conquering London, felt awkward and provincial. He felt how different the English were. The shyness and sense of aloneness he had experienced in Dublin returned more strongly than before. He had arrived at the foot of the mountain he had vowed to climb. Now he realised how little he was equipped to do it; how improbable it was that he ever would.

For an indigent young intellectual with time on his hands, London had plenty to offer for free. The British Museum and the National Gallery became haunts of Shaw's, and he dipped into his small budget to attend concerts and lectures. Lucy had made friends with people in artistic and literary circles. At this time she was at the height of her promise as a singer, and dressed to enhance her resemblance to the famous actress Ellen Terry. Oscar Wilde's mother, the Irish poet 'Speranza', was living in London and it was at a party given by her that Shaw – brought along by Lucy – first met Oscar Wilde.

Neither Lucy nor his mother had much sympathy with Shaw's proclaimed aim to become a writer. They thought he should take up some form of regular employment, and after the first few weeks of his stay, there was much nagging at him to go and find a job. They had become accustomed to the notion of Sonny the office-worker. Largely to humour them, he went to one or two interviews, but was offered nothing. He bought a teach-yourself French course, but found at the end of it that he could not speak French. Still under domestic pressure, he went to a 'crammer's' teaching establishment to swot up for the entrance examination to the Customs and Excise Service, but withdrew himself when Vandeleur Lee, once the enemy who had had him consigned to that unmentionable school, offered him some work. Lee was now a busy man, with a flat in Park Lane, seeking his clientele in the most fashionable part of London. He was also supposed to be music critic of a weekly paper, *The Hornet,* but could not find the time. Knowing Shaw's writerly ambition, and aware of his knowledge of music, he offered Shaw a deal – the young man would do the criticisms, and receive half the (very modest) pay. In addition, Lee offered some work in his Park Lane school. With this tenuous line towards his future ambition in his hand, Shaw renounced the Customs and Excise, quitting the crammer's in mid-course without regret.

The Hornet was not destined for long life, and disappeared in October 1877. Shaw did odd jobs for Lee, largely putting Lee's notes into readable English for pamphlets produced to explain or promote his teaching. Lee however was not a long-term prospect. He did not possess the necessary manner or charm of a Mayfair music-master, and though he accommodated 'The Method' to a short-term learning course for London young ladies, his clientele began to dwindle. By the time he died in 1886, Mrs Shaw had long since parted with him and was running her own kind of music teaching with steady industry and success.

Meanwhile her son had set himself to becoming a novelist. From March to September 1879, writing a regular 1500 words a day for over 200 days, he completed a long novel entitled *Immaturity*. It was rejected by half a dozen publishers, though Shaw claimed that one, Blackwood, took the book on, and then dropped it. The most considered opinion on his manuscript came to him from Macmillan, possibly from their reader John Morley, later the liberal peer and author Lord Morley. It acknowledged qualities of humour and realism but essentially found the text dry, plotless, unemotional, and much too long.

Undeterred, Shaw began work on a second novel. His sister Lucy meantime maintained her stream of criticism of his apparently idle ways and nagged at him to find a paying job. She even tried to enlist his friend McNulty to help persuade him into the path of responsibility. It may have been at her behest that George Shaw obtained from Uniacke Townshend a testimonial to his son, two years after Shaw's resignation. It was a handsome tribute to his reliability and integrity, but Shaw was angered by the interference. Lucy herself was not earning anything. Mrs Shaw's earnings, plus her very small inherited income, paid for the household. But Mrs Shaw was also in charge of a bequest from her mother's father of £4,000, to be used for the benefit of her children when they attained the age of twenty-one, and she appears to have used this – not unreasonably perhaps – to help in supporting her musical daughter and her literary son. Other relatives contributed to the harassing of the young man into employment. His cousin, Fanny Johnstone (who herself was a published novelist) arranged for him to be introduced to the manager of the London branch of the Edison Telephone Company. Driven by these pressures, Shaw joined Edison's as an apprentice telephone engineer in November 1879; despite the title, his role turned out to be that of a field-worker, arranging for the erection of telephone posts on private property. Telephones were perhaps more acceptable to the young Shaw than banking or estate agencies. The telephone was still very new, and beginning to revolutionize the way in which business was done. Shaw was always to be an enthusiast for new inventions and mechanical devices. But knocking on doors and haggling with reluctant or greedy property-owners was not so very different from collecting rents. Shaw stuck it for six months, then resigned, partly because he found the income would not suffice to keep him (although at £48 plus commission on successful results, it was better than the zero which was the alternative). The response of the telephone company was to promote him, and he was in charge of the wayleave department by June 1880. At that time the Edison and Bell telephone companies were merged, and though Shaw was offered a post in the combined business, he finally did resign, and devoted himself again entirely to his ambition.

The long, unrewarded and constantly domestically criticised apprenticeship which Shaw served as a fiction writer reveals both tenacity and will-power, which, in different ways, his parents had also shown themselves capable of. It also displays a lack of self-judgement and of any sense of his own direction. Shaw was to write five novels, all of them refused by the publishing industry, and to embark on a sixth, before he gave up the thought of storming the world as a fiction writer. Every morning he wrote 1,500 words. The approach was an almost mechanistic one, as though he could turn himself on, like a machine, and produce the desired length, texture and quality within a set time. It took him nine years to write these novels, during which time his earnings were minimal. It was not until he had achieved fame in other ways that his novels were issued. The aptly named *Immaturity* was followed by *The Irrational Knot, The Unsocial Socialist, Love Among the Artists* and *Cashel Byron's Profession*. The novels are not easy reading, as their author never mastered the art of plot and character development which a novel requires. Nor was he setting out, as his younger contemporary James Joyce would, to revolutionize the novel form. Shaw's novels reflect more the spirit of the clever person who reads a novel and says: 'I can do that', and proceeds to produce a laborious and long-winded effort which, while it shows the cleverness and hints at the abilities of the writer, completely fails both as a story and as a work of literature. Shaw is quoted, in *Days With Bernard Shaw* by Stephen Winsten, as saying of a novel by George Eliot: 'I could do that sort of writing, I thought.' Unfortunately, he was quite wrong. His work on the novels was to bear some fruit in his mastery of dialogue and ability to render character through a few words of speech, but it was a high price to pay for a skill that might have emerged much sooner.

Those first London years were grim ones in many ways for Shaw. He was conscious of his ability but had not yet found the means of expressing it effectively. He was tolerated by his mother, with no encouragement or interest in his ambition; his presence infuriated his sister, who frequently told his mother she should throw him out. He had few friends. McNulty, his soul-mate of earlier days, was still in Dublin. To maintain his confidence in himself, to churn out his 1,500 words each day, was a struggle. As a boy in a home where little affection was given, he had already learned a degree of self-sufficiency and to cover up his sense of emotional deprivation. St John Ervine wrote that though he: '… took great trouble throughout his life to pretend that he was superior to common affection and ordinary human feeling, he was intensely emotional, full of affection and eager to possess it …' – but the lean and unproductive years forced him to adopt even more of a front, to face the uncaring or critical world with a don't-care jauntiness and a barrage of words intended to deflect attention from his own inner self. In appearance and presence he was no shrinking violet; he had become a striking figure of a man, over six feet tall, with an imposing face. His hair was reddish, parted in the centre, and he had grown a frizzy, jutting beard. The strength of his features, verging on cragginess even in his twenties, was lightened by his eyes, bright blue, lively, sharply observant, full of mischief and penetration, which still look out from all the many portraits he sat for.

The most valuable effect of his writing at this time was that it forced him to think, and to reflect on his own ideas, and to look for ways of developing them, and also to look for people who shared them. Ever since his acquaintance with Chichester Bell in Dublin, he had been interested in one particular aspect of language. This was phonetics, the means by which speech sounds can be accurately set down. The extraordinary illogicality of English pronunciation bothered Shaw throughout his life. He was deeply interested in the origin and formation of alphabets, and became a crusader for the reform of English spelling and pronunciation. In these interests, and also in his love of music, he found a friend, James Lecky, an expert on musical instruments. Lecky had numerous friends who shared his own interests in a whole range of social issues, and in late 1879 he brought the twenty-four-year-old Shaw to a meeting of the Zetetical Society. The society was a forum for intellectuals with progressive views on life and society – cranks, reformers, idealists and eccentrics – in which the young writer immediately felt at home. He was with kindred spirits, but still deeply unsure of himself. His first public speech was made to the Zetetical Society. Shaw records his feelings as tremulous in the extreme:

'I suffered agonies that no-one suspected. During the speech of the debate that I resolved to follow, my heart used to beat as painfully as a recruit's going under fire for the first time. I could not use notes; when I looked at the paper in my hand I could not collect myself enough to decipher a word. And of the four or five wretched points that were my pretext for this ghastly practice of mine, I invariably forgot three – the best three.'

Shaw wrote this much later to his American biographer Professor Archibald Henderson, and the tone of self-deprecation, with the favourite word 'wretched', should warn the reader against taking it too literally. Shaw is also saying at the same time that he was capable of speaking in public without notes, a gift denied to those who do not feel some confidence. And at the third meeting he attended, he was invited to take the chair. His doubts and agonies were genuine enough, but they took place far beneath the surface and were only part of the picture. Shaw knew that he could do it.

Among the members of the Zetetical Society (the name means 'Society of Seekers') was Sidney Webb, a clerk in the Colonial Office, who was three years younger than Shaw. His father was an accountant, and he was studying for a law degree at London University. Webb and Shaw had little in common physically; Sidney was a small man with slight limbs and a very large, round head. George Bernard was tall and rangy with a large, long head. But their ideas on society coincided, and a lifelong friendship and alliance developed between them. Webb's capacious brain excelled in statistics and records. Economics and sociology were his chosen field, and as main founder of the London School of Economics and Political Science (1895), he would combine these interests in an institution which played a large part in British political thought in the twentieth century. The discussions and formal debates of the Zeteticals brought Shaw into an area where social thought and social movement were acting on one another with increasing speed and effect. The urban population of England had grown dramatically in the course of the century. The working classes, concentrated in towns and cities in huge numbers, was beginning to become organised. Trade unions, once banned, were gaining members steadily. Electoral reform gave the vote to men over twenty-one. It also began to alter the parliamentary constituencies, so that each was of approximately similar population size. The workers' votes began to have a major importance. But there was not, as yet, a workers' political party to represent their interests. The two great parties of the times, Tories and Liberals, both mainly represented, with different emphases and attitudes, the owners of the country's wealth, broadly speaking the landed interest on the one side, and industry and commerce on the other. Despite many reforms, there was still great and manifest inequality in the country. Administration was still very old-fashioned, designed for the England of several generations ago; and in the case of Ireland, centuries ago. The extremely poor vastly outnumbered the extremely rich, though the extremely rich owned most of the nation's resources. To the percipient, however much things had changed, they would have to change further. Progressives wanted to harness and direct the forces of change. Reactionaries wanted to curb them. Shaw flung himself eagerly into this current of political, economic and social issues, on the progressive side.

His mission was a wholly progressive one, to awaken the workers to their own power and to the correct vision of their future. But in one respect he did not share the views of most of his associates. Then and later, he had little time for the trade unions. He disliked their participation in politics and their regimentation of their members. Shaw's political world was composed of inviduals who would see the light and act on their own behalf, in the best interest of the community. It was far removed from the dour pragmatism of the trade union leaders, still welding their new and unaccustomed thousands of members into a movement where 'Solidarity' was the prime essential in the face of the entrenched, crafty and unremittingly hostile forces of Capital.

In 1881 Mrs Shaw moved house to Fitzroy Street, just north of central London, and her son moved with her. In January of this year, Shaw also became a vegetarian, and remained one for the rest of his life. He was a regular sufferer from headaches, and hoped that a meat-free diet would alleviate them (it did not). In May, he contracted smallpox. Despite the vaccine that had been available for eighty years, this disease was still endemic. As its treatment required isolation, and he remained at home, it must have been a sore test of his mother's regard for him, since she too would have been unable to go out in public. But Mrs Shaw, if she did not dispense love and tenderness, did her duty. After three weeks of illness, Shaw went to convalesce at his uncle Walter's. Mrs Shaw's brother had retired from the sea and was working as a doctor in East London.

Ill and vulnerable to family pressure, Shaw again considered paid employment, and even thought of emigrating to the United States. But nothing came of it. He continued to write, by now engaged in *Love Among the Artists*. In 1882, they moved to Osnaburgh Street, in the Bayswater district of London. Lucy had joined a professional music group, the

Carl Rosa Opera Company, but he remained dependent. He regarded his mother, if not with love, then with understanding, writing later, again with his own self-deprecatory twist to the tale:

'I did not throw myself into the struggle for life: I threw my mother into it ... I steadily wrote my five pages a day (at my mother's expense) ... My mother worked for my living instead of preaching at me to work for hers.'

– from the preface to *The Irrational Knot*. When Shaw began earning money, he looked after his mother well. His diary from 1882 records how he and she played card games like euchre together, as well as chess. Mother and son were closer perhaps in his twenties than at any previous or later time.

Interest in matters social and political led Shaw to attend a talk given by a visiting American, Henry George, in September 1882. George, the apostle of a land tax which he claimed would make all other taxes unnecessary, and eradicate, or nearly eradicate, poverty, was on a lecture tour of Britain, speaking to packed halls and enthusiastic audiences. A charismatic figure and powerful orator, with a touch of prophetic inspiration, he was however no demagogue, but a man of strongly humane values. Shaw was greatly impressed by both the man and his speech. He bought a copy of George's book *Progress and Poverty* and read it with great care. It was a significant book for Shaw, though George's impact on his ideas was overshadowed in the end by Marx, whose *Capital* he read, in the following year, using a French translation, in the same British Museum Reading Room where Marx had written it. Shaw's political ideas were sufficiently thought out, and his enthusiasm sufficiently great, to turn him into a public orator. He had discovered and joined other societies and groups, including the Land Reform Union and the Social Democratic Federation. His range of friends of 'advanced views' had grown wider, and he was much more keen on their company than on the arty people he met with Lucy at Lady Wilde's soirées and other musical occasions.

In 1882 Shaw began his first recorded love affair, when in March he began writing playfully amorous verses to Alice Lockett, a nurse who was one of his mother's music pupils. In September 1883 he escorted Alice from Osnaburgh Street to Liverpool Street Station, and made some sort of overture to her which appears to have alarmed or offended her, and he wrote to apologise and explain himself:

'. . . in playing on my own thoughts for the most charming of companions last night, I unskilfully struck a note that pained her . . . The heart of any other man would have stopped during those seconds after you had slowly turned your back upon the barrier and yet were still in doubt. Mine is a machine and did not stop; but it did something strange. It put me in *suspense,* which is the essence of woman's power over man, and which you had never made me feel before . . . Believe nothing that I say – and I have a wicked tongue, a deadly pen, and a cold heart – I shall be angry with myself tomorrow for sending you this, and yet, when I meet you, I shall plunge into fresh cause for danger . . . Do not read it. Alas! it is too late: you have read it.

G. B. S.'

It is a fascinating letter, in its mixture of guarded emotional admission – he does not mention what the cause of her annoyance was – of self-praise and self-dismissal; in his comparison of himself, especially his heart, with a machine; in the clever posturing even when he is pleading for forgiveness. Alice Lockett must have had some difficulty in evaluating the writer's sincerity. This problem would be shared by many of Shaw's correspondents. The direct, simple expression of deep and genuine personal feeling was something that he could not achieve. Like watching for a trout in the ripples, it took a keen eye to see through the changing pattern and discern if there was something there beneath the surface, or only a trick of the light. No wonder Alice claimed he was not serious; to which he replied: 'If you have made me feel, have I not made you think?'

The somewhat cerebral passion for Alice gradually dwindled, though they did not lose touch for some years. She eventually married a doctor, and, partly because she remained friendly with Mrs Shaw (as many of her pupils did), more than ten years later she brought her husband to Mrs Shaw's and insisted on his examining Shaw. She was convinced he had tuberculosis, but her husband could detect nothing of any significance.

In October 1885 Shaw and Alice were still meeting and exchanging letters. But in the course of that year another woman had entered his life. This was Jenny Patterson, again a pupil of his mother's. She was older than Alice, and fifteen years older than Shaw; a widow of some wealth, who lived at a fashionable address in Brompton Square. From February of that year she became worthy of note in Shaw's diary, with brief records of contact, including visits to her house. One of these contains the comment, 'Virgo intacta still': the reference is to himself. From July 26th, the date of his twenty-ninth birthday, the description was no longer applicable. Shaw's comments on his affair with Mrs Patterson are clouded by the rancour with which their relationship ended; no letters between them have been preserved. He referred to their first sexual encounter as a 'rape' on her part, adding to his diary: 'I was an absolute novice. I did not take the initiative in the matter.' She was a lively, hot-blooded woman of forty-four and may have employed a brusque and no-nonsense approach to getting the talkative, shy, virginal, uncertain young Irishman into her bed. For a time, they saw each other with great frequency, and his diary records a succession of late-night or early morning departures from her house. Jenny Patterson's intentions are not known: whether she merely ventured into a romantic and passionate affair or whether she had hopes of marriage, even of children. Shaw later flung accusations of promiscuity and nymphomania at her: once he called at her house when an unknown man was there; each tried to sit the other out, but Shaw won. But there is no doubt that she was extremely possessive of him. At this time, quite apart from the not-quite dead relationship with Alice, Shaw had newly met three other women to whom he was strongly attracted. One was May Morris, the daughter of William Morris, another was Florence Farr, needlewoman and actress. The third was Annie Besant. They were all remarkable women, more so than Jenny, whose jealousy was easily aroused and led her to far from lady-like behaviour.

The diary in which Shaw noted these encounters was not a document to which he unburdened his heart. The entries are brief and sporadic, with long gaps. It provides the record of a frugal life. When he noted his daily expenditure, every halfpenny was accounted for. A typical day would show (in the coinage of the time) 3d on Underground train fares, a shilling on a vegetarian lunch, with a penny tip recorded separately, a penny-halfpenny on postage stamps. He was careful with his money because he had to be, but he was not parsimonious. Pennies given to begging children are noted. Later, when he was a rich man, Shaw was usually generous both to individuals and causes that took his sympathy.

Early in 1883 Shaw made friends with a fellow-user of the British Museum's Reading Room, William Archer, a Scot by birth, and of the same age as himself, but who unlike Shaw had travelled widely. He was keenly interested in the contemporary theatre, and while in Italy he had met the famous Norwegian dramatist Henrik Ibsen. Ibsen (1828–1906) was in self-imposed exile from his native Norway and writing his great dramas of irony and realism, exposing the shams and hollowness so often found behind the screen of conventional life. Archer had written a book called *English Dramatists of Today,* was drama critic of the magazine *The World,* and contributed reviews and articles to other papers. It was Archer's theatrical interests that awoke Shaw, still toiling on his last novel, to the possibilities of theatre. But Archer, a generous though always candid friend, also directed numerous commissions towards Shaw, helping to increase his income and making him better known to editors and readers.

Shaw's Socialist and Communist friends knew of his

novel-writing, and some of them had been allowed to read the carefully written manuscript notebooks. As a result of this, Henry Hyde Champion, editor of a progressive political magazine, *Today,* offered to publish the novels in serial form. The finances of the journal did not run to payment, but Shaw was happy to see his work given a platform. *Today* serialised *An Unsocial Socialist* through 1884, and this resulted in an offer for book publication by Swan, Sonnenschein, who duly published it to appreciative reviews, though its sales were very modest. The magazine serial had also been read by William Morris, the wealthy poet and craftsman, founder of the Arts and Crafts movement, and one of the fathers of the Labour Party, and he sought out the author. The friendship with Morris was to lead to some crucial moments in Shaw's life.

At the start of 1884, and by a geographical coincidence in Osnaburgh Street, where Shaw also lived, the Fabian Society was founded. Its aim was to work for social improvement, and its name was borrowed from the Roman general Fabius Cunctator ('The Delayer'), whose delaying tactics against Hannibal were criticised by the Senate, but who proved to have been biding his time, to strike all the harder at the opportune moment. Shaw picked up one of the Fabians' first leaflets, *Why Are the Many Poor?* and was impressed. In September 1884 he became a member of the Society, wrote its second pamphlet, *A Manifesto,* and also introduced his friend Sidney Webb, who joined in April 1885. They immediately became leading figures in what was numerically a very small body, though it was to prove highly influential. Shaw's manifesto had demanded, among other things, full political rights for women, the equal division of wealth, and State provision of 'happy homes for children', not for orphan children but those who needed a refuge against the tyranny or neglect of their 'natural custodians' – a provision that perhaps seemed more vital to him than to many of his readers.

CHAPTER IV

THE PHILANDERER

In some circles, albeit limited ones, Shaw was becoming a man to notice. Attendance at many debates had sharpened his skill as a public speaker and polemicist. Unexpectedly perhaps for those who saw him as an impassioned orator, he also showed great gifts as a committee-man. Whilst many of the people who had the opportunity to see him in action were rank and file members of the various societies, never to be famous, a few were destined to become public figures themselves. Sidney Webb was one such, as was his wife Beatrice, whom he met in 1890. Graham Wallas, later to be Professor of Political Science at London University and author of *The Great Society,* was another. Annie Besant was already a celebrity when she joined the Fabian Society and encountered Shaw.

Mrs Besant at that time was an atheist, though later she would become a mystic, and end up as the leader of the Theosophical Society. Most of the Fabians shared her anti-religious views, Shaw among them. Among intellectuals there was considerable interest in the occult, which was a high fashion in Paris. Shaw was drawn into this on one occasion, but refused to take it seriously. Frank Podmore, the chairman of the Fabians, was a member of the Society for Psychical Research and on one occasion Shaw went with him and some others to sleep in an allegedly haunted house; and on another occasion he and the journalist H. W. Massingham rigged a 'table-turning' session, causing the spirit presences to: 'rap out long stories, lift the table, and finally drink tumblers of whisky and water' and noting sardonically that their spiritualist colleague Ernest Bax was completely taken in by their antics. Unlike Yeats, who was an enthusiastic inquirer into the 'spirit world', Shaw's universe was essentially a material one; though he believed it to be driven by a non-material 'Life-Force', he had no time for the astrological charts, tarot cards, drug-induced trances and spirit-interviews that captivated many otherwise intelligent people.

His thirtieth year was an eventful and stormy one. No longer the solitary walker, Shaw began to impinge on other people's lives. William Morris's enthusiasm for *An Unsocial Socialist* brought Shaw invitations to Kelmscott House, Morris's handsome riverside home in Hammersmith, West London. It was the nerve-centre of Morris's multifarious interests, artistic, political and commercial, and a correspondingly wide range of visitors came. Morris's daughter May ran an embroidery workshop from the house. Through 1886 his relationship with Jenny Patterson continued, but from the laconic evidence of his diary, he was finding it more of a trouble than a blessing. Mrs Patterson was a woman of strong feelings, which included a strong temper, and it took little to make the temper flare up. Shaw had no desire to be possessed, or to be railed at, by an angry virago. During 1886 he began to request that their affair should become a platonic one. But the liaison continued for several years; it was 1893 before a final break was made.

For almost eight years this 'tempestuous petticoat', as he referred to her, clung obstinately to her increasingly luke-warm, reluctant and wayward lover. Jenny played little part in his political or social life. She remained a family friend, on close terms with Mrs Shaw and Lucy. The family had moved from Osnaburgh Street to Fitzroy Square, and on at least one occasion, Jenny came to stay at with them there, plaguing Shaw, who wanted to get on with his work. The British Museum became a refuge from Jenny, who used her friend-ship with the Shaw women to call whenever she felt ne-glected by him or threatened by his friendships with other women: 'J. P. came, raged, wept, flung a book at my head etc.' wrote Shaw in one of his oddly dispassionate diary notes. The same diary contains references to listlessness, headaches, and depression at this time, a sense of malaise which could have had several causes, including his late-night habits; he was often up late, either because of post-concert meals or other engagements, or because of his writing. Two in the morning was often the time at which he went to bed.

The other women who entered into his life came from his new political and literary connections. They were intellec-tual friends and spiritual mates, and in some cases the rela-tionship never went beyond this stage, which does not mean that it lacked commitment or intensity. Shaw was after all a man of the mind above all. He loved to commune with women. His nature, responsive, genial, ultimately self-pro-tective, thrived in a climate of feminine interest and admira-tion, and also, in its combination of vulnerability and remoteness, seems to have attracted sensitive and perceptive women. Several such relationships could be indulged in at the same time, in a degree of promiscuity that would be dangerous, if not impossible, in a sexual partnership – as Jenny was always there to remind him by her presence and her behaviour. The writer Frank Harris, who wrote an early biography of Shaw which speculated fairly crudely on his sexuality and sex life, said that he was the only man who cut a swathe through the theatre and left it strewn with virgins.

Early in 1885 Shaw was invited to lecture to one of the many progressive groups that were formed and vanished again around this time. This was the Dialectical Society, and his subject was Socialism. Some time before, he had incurred the anger of Mrs Annie Besant by going into print to oppose her claim for custody of her children, in the bitter divorce suit against her clergyman husband. Mrs Besant had left him and associated herself with the militant Radical politician and atheist Charles Bradlaugh. They had compounded their sin by becoming public advocates of birth control. Shaw had no objection to their beliefs, but he had strong views about child-rearing and did not consider Mrs Besant's hectic life-style, with its travels and evening meetings, a good one for young children. Mrs Besant had become a formidable orator and debater, and Shaw suffered more than the usual trepidation when he knew she was to be in the audience for his lecture. Mrs Besant was friendly however, and soon she and Shaw were on good terms. It was he who supported her request to join the Fabians. She became a patron of his, serialising two of his novels, *The Irrational Knot* and *Love Among the Artists,* between 1885 and 1888, in her magazine *Our Corner,* the organ of the National Secular Society. But she paid Shaw out of her own funds; when he discovered this he refused further payment. There were many occasions to meet Mrs Besant under the auspices of the Fabians or other groups; and Shaw also went with her to concerts. She shared his love of music and they would play duets on her piano. They also exchanged frequent letters, but at Christmas 1886 they returned each other's letters. This was the conventional action when a love affair terminated. Shaw noted:

'The intimacy with Mrs Besant alluded to last year reached in January a point at which it threatened to become a vulgar intrigue, chiefly through my fault ... At Christmas, I returned all her letters and she mine. Reading over my letters before destroying them, rather disgusted me with my trifling of the last two years over women.'

A few weeks before that Christmas, Jenny Patterson, snooping through his papers, had discovered some of Annie Besant's letters to Shaw, and a tremendous scene resulted. Around this same time, he detected Jenny following him and Mrs Besant in the street. Between Jenny's bombardings and his own almost instinctive recoil from deep involvement, the closeness between Shaw and Annie Besant never was physically consummated and never came to a full relationship. Afterwards they would remain friends, and co-workers for the cause, but no more than that.

Shaw had been converted to Communism by a book, *Capital.* Marx's thesis seemed to him thoroughly logical.

Partly at least because it was as much an intellectual conclusion as a spiritual ideal, he remained faithful to it all his life. It had little to do with experience or Communism in practice. But in November 1887 he found himself for a moment at the raw, real and bloody edge of politics. It was a time of industrial slump, and unemployment was high. Wages were being reduced and working conditions made harder, by companies struggling to survive. Shaw and his colleagues across the motley range of small pressure-groups, agitatory cells and trade union bosses which had not yet been forged into the Labour Party, did not agree with such survival being at the expense of the workers rather than the shareholders. A great march was organized, converging on Trafalgar Square from several different directions, despite a police ban on meeting there. Shaw addressed one contingent, at Clerkenwell Green, pleading for resolution and discipline. Mrs Besant was with him. Their section got as far as Bloomsbury to find there was already a violent confrontation going on in central London: police and demonstrators were engaged in a battle that gave the whole episode the name of 'Bloody Sunday'. Shaw urged Mrs Besant to flee, which she did. The marchers were dispersed by police tactics, with many claims of indiscriminate violence. The whole event was a severe shock to Shaw. He loathed and was alarmed by violence, and he was one of those who won the argument against repeating the demonstration. In popular legend he was said to be 'the first man to run away from Trafalgar Square on Bloody Sunday', but Shaw, admitting in his disarming way that he was a physical coward, said that the story flattered him, because he had not had even that much sense.

William Morris had converted the coach-house of his home to a small lecture-hall, and Shaw gave several talks there. It was at a party at Morris's in 1888 that he first met W. B. Yeats, who had been introduced to Morris in Dublin, and renewed the acquaintance in London. Yeats, at the height of his youthful earnestness and developing his own high-minded poetic persona, thought his fellow-Dubliner a shallow-minded fellow. He wrote to his friend Katharine Tynan:

'... last night at Morris's I met Bernard Shaw, who is certainly very witty. But, like most people who have wit rather than humour, his mind is maybe somewhat lacking in depth. However, his stories are good, they say.'

– the implication is that Shaw's growing fame had reached back to his native city, or at least to those residents who took an interest in literary affairs. Shaw himself must have met Morris's daughter May on numerous occasions, but on one such meeting, he was smitten in a strange fashion:

'One Sunday evening after lecturing and supping, I was on the threshold of the Hammersmith house when I turned to make my farewell, and at that moment she came from the dining room into the hall. I looked at her, rejoicing in the lovely dress and lovely self; and she looked at me very carefully and quite deliberately made a gesture of assent with her eyes. I was immediately conscious that a Mystic Betrothal was registered in heaven, to be fulfilled when all the material obstacles should melt away, and my own position rescued

65

from the squalor of my poverty and unsuccess; for subconsciously I had no doubt of my rank as a man of genius ... I did not think it necessary to say anything ... It did not occur to me even that fidelity to the Mystical Betrothal need interfere with the ordinary course of my relations with other women.'

– Once again the reader, trying to get to the bottom of what this extraordinary man really felt, meets a whole series of baffles and excuses. Did he really feel that his poverty was an obstacle, or did he make it into one? It is plain that Shaw was not a 'red-blooded' male of the Frank Harris type, who would have interpreted the look in Miss Morris's eyes in quite a different way and promptly swept her off to some secluded couch, damning any notion of a mystic marriage for a much more physical union. Thin-blooded by comparison, and suffering from any number of mental doubts and self-mortifications about each additional attachment, Shaw was nevertheless carrying on light-hearted flirtations, with half a dozen different women at this time. It is notable that he was still living in his mother's house – not the best base for a Casanova, and even when he could afford to move out, he did not. But, as he acknowledged later, what to him may have been little more than a game, and perhaps also some sort of gesture of defiance in the direction of the succubus-figure of Jenny in her lair in Brompton Square, ended up as a painful reality to those who were its victims. May Morris was the chief of these.

Whilst Shaw nursed his mystical betrothal with her, she contracted the more normal kind of engagement with

Henry Sparling, an associate of Morris's circle who seems to have been regarded by just about everyone as an objectionable little man. Shaw was taken by surprise and shock; tired anyway by overwork, late nights, nervous excitement and the demands of Jenny, he managed to install himself with the newly wedded couple: 'She was glad to have me in the house; and he was glad to have me because I kept her in good humour.' His presence wrecked the doomed marriage. Sparling soon abandoned May and ran away to France. May Morris was left with neither her husband nor her mystic groom. Shaw went blithely on with his own life, which for some time had included the relationship which his liaison with Jenny Patterson finally wrecked. By a further irony, this relationship, with Florence Farr, began when he met Florence as one of May Morris's workroom staff.

The intrusion of the emotionally raw young man into the life of another couple had a parallel at much the same time in his links with the actress Janet Achurch and her husband Charles Charrington, also an actor. Achurch was an intellectual actress who had played Ibsen parts. Shaw's devotion to her lasted a long time, but the easy-going and improvident Charrington accepted it (and Shaw's occasional financial help) without making a fuss. Shaw gained a reputation as a philanderer, a trifler with woman. As a consequence, the aunt of Grace Gilchrist, a young lady Fabian to whom he had begun to pay attention, waged a campaign against him that culminated in a public confrontation outside his haven of the British Museum, causing him to stop pursuing Miss Gilchrist. It is hard not to form the view that Shaw, having emerged belatedly from the shell of maternal rejection, of

67

work and relative poverty, had no idea how to conduct himself with the female sex. Liking attractive, clever women, not driven by a strong sexual urge, fundamentally uncaring about – or perhaps unable to believe in – his effect upon their feelings, he was happy to drift into any number of relationships without putting his full heart into any of them. There is no doubt that such women were attracted to him. One of them was E. (for Edith) Nesbit, whose reputation as a superb writer for children has outlived her Fabian activities. She had a considerable crush on Shaw, but though he became her friend, he did not let matters develop into even an intellectual love affair, perhaps because she was married to another Fabian, the polygamous Hubert Bland (Bland was an aggressive personality who shared Shaw's own interest in boxing). E. Nesbit described the Shaw of 1885 as:

'. . . a very clever writer and speaker – is the grossest flatterer (of men, women and children impartially) I ever met, is horribly untrustworthy as he repeats everything he hears, and does not always stick to the truth . . . and yet is one of the most fascinating men I ever met. Everyone rather affects to despise him. "Oh, it's only Shaw". That sort of thing, you know, but everyone admires him all the same.'

– and this was at a time when Shaw had yet to prove himself to be the great man that his subconscious mind already knew him to be. Those who knew him expected great things from him.

In April 1885 his father died, aged seventy-one. The London-based Shaw family took the event calmly, and did not go to Dublin to attend the modest funeral. He had come to London once to visit Lucinda; none of them had gone to visit him. A modest insurance payment of about £100 duly made its way to Mrs Shaw, who passed some of it on to her son to buy clothes. From now on, clothing joined the other interests, phonetics and spelling reform, vegetarianism, bicycle riding and long walks, which gave Shaw the reputation, which he relished and cultivated, of being a crank. On his Dublin salary, he had been well-dressed in a conventional way, with hand-made suits, including an evening suit. Now he made his way to Jaeger, and purchased an all-wool suit, together with cravat and collars, his first new clothes for a long time.

Among Socialist groups, he was in demand as an orator. Shaw travelled considerable distances to address meetings in halls and gatherings in public places. This was unpaid activity, but thanks to his friend Archer, he had become the art critic of *The World,* and a book reviewer for the *Pall Mall Gazette.* His name was becoming known, as a journalist, to readers who knew nothing about his personal life. Archer also suggested to Shaw that they might collaborate in writing a play. Archer felt that he could supply a plot, but knew he could not write dialogue. Shaw's novels, which he had read, showed that Shaw could write sparkling dialogue (and also that he was no master of plot construction). This apparently perfect combination of talents did not survive in practice. Shaw seized upon Archer's plot sketch, disposed of it in the first act, and demanded more. Archer was astonished and somewhat at a loss – he thought he had supplied the structure of the entire play. In the end he gracefully withdrew from the collaboration, and Shaw, with much else to do, laid the work aside. Another prompt in the direction of plays came from the publishers Swan, Sonnenschein, who had failed to make money out of his novel *An Unsocial Socialist,* but whose editor, not at all discouraged, suggested that plays would be even more suited to Shaw's talent than novels.

CHAPTER

V

EMERGENCE OF THE PLAYWRIGHT

In January 1888 Shaw was recruited to the staff of a new London evening newspaper, *The Star*, on the recommendation of his friend H.W. Massingham, who was its deputy editor. The editor was a fellow-Irishman, T. P. O'Connor, known – though not in his hearing – as 'Tay Pay', who was also an Irish Nationalist member of the Westminster Parliament. Shaw's political writings very soon proved to be altogether too revolutionary for O'Connor and he resigned, to be immediately reinstated, at his own suggestion, as the music critic. His salary, a little more than £100 a year, was not great, but the work allowed him considerable free time for his other interests and activities, it suited his night-bird inclinations, and provided him with a steady stream of concerts to which he could take his numerous lady friends. He was still art critic of *The World,* but resigned in 1889 when the owner began to interfere with his texts and asked him to be kind to the artists who were her friends.

In his brief earlier spell as a music reviewer, devilling for Vandeleur Lee, Shaw had earned the enmity of concert promoters by the scathing nature of his criticism. Now his tone was more relaxed and confident. Though his criticism could be fierce, it was tempered by humour. He took the pseudonym of 'Corno di Bassetto', an obsolete instrument, forerunner of the clarinet, perhaps because it reminded him that he had once briefly aspired to be a professional cornet player. He took up his job with great enthusiasm:

'I took care that Corno di Bassetto should always be amusing and, by using knowledge, to provide a solid substratum of genuine criticism.'

It was the undoubted musical knowledge of the pseudonymous critic that made his flamboyantly delivered judgements respected even when the professionals and performers were infuriated, and later made the articles worth collecting into three published volumes, *Music In London, 1890–94*. He damned and praised in memorable language. Corno di Bassetto, who put his own ebullient personality across in no uncertain way, was read for entertainment by people with no interest in music:

'The artist who accounts for my disparagement by alleging personal animosity is quite right: when people do less than their best, and do that less at once badly and self-complacently, I hate them, loathe them, long to tear them limb from limb and strew them in gobbets about the stage or platform.'

Here is a favourite Shavian literary trick at work. The remarks seem to be promising an astonishing confession – the critic really is prompted by personal malice – only to turn it round triumphantly to show that it is only bad art and un-warranted self-satisfaction that he hates, and who does not? The point is made humorously, and the shocking violence of the language, set in the decorous context of the concert-hall, becomes humorous as well.

The reader of his musical criticisms and political writings is left with the thought that Shaw might have been an inspired teacher. The enthusiasm, the infectious energy, the memorable phrases, the way in which his presentation forces the listener or reader to pay attention – all these are hallmarks of the great teacher. But Shaw was always writing for, or addressing, an audience. He did not possess the sympathetic interest in helping unpromising individuals which a good teacher has (although he would go to great trouble with favoured individuals, such as Erica Cotterill – of whom more later – he was more prone to dispense advice than to give detailed teaching). His skills however did make him a superb propagandist.

Corno di Bassetto brought a fresh vision to musical criticism. He reported on Salvation Army bands – favourably – and on street buskers and amateur performances, as well as on the usual run of concerts and celebrity events. He criticised audiences:

'. . . when every possible excuse is made for the people who coughed, it remains a matter for regret that the attendants did not remove them to Piccadilly, and treat their ailment there by gently passing a warm steam-roller over their chests.'

His sister Lucy, who had for years been an acerbic critic of his apparent indolence and hopeless ambition, suffered a review of her performance in the musical comedy 'Dorothy':

'Dorothy herself, a beauteous young lady of distinguished mien ... sang without the slightest effort and without the slightest point, and was all the more desperately vapid because she suggested artistic gifts wasting in complacent abeyance.'

This was a sharp reversal of roles. It was true that Lucy Shaw, despite her fine voice and long training, never achieved what was expected of her as a singer, largely because she was incapable of projecting a warm stage personality. She had married, and though the marriage was a failure and ended in divorce, she continued to live with her in-laws.

At the start of 1890, Shaw left *The Star* to rejoin *The World* as its music critic, at double the money. He had just seen the publication of a volume of *Fabian Essays,* edited by himself, in December 1889. The first edition of a thousand copies sold out almost on publication, a remarkable achievement for a society whose membership was only about 150 people. Further editions followed, including low-priced paperback versions. The contributors, apart from Shaw himself, included Mrs Besant, Sidney Webb and Graham Wallas. The volume played an important role among thinking people in preparing the ground for the Labour Party: in 1892 the first Labour member was elected to the Westminster Parliament. His friend Sidney Webb married in 1892, creating the formidable combination, with his wife Beatrice, of 'The Webbs': joint authors of major politico-socio-economic books. Beatrice Webb did not greatly care for Shaw, whom she considered frivolous and lightweight – 'a sprite' was her term for him. Her interest in social engineering extended to manipulation of the lives of her friends, but Shaw was too elusive for her, though she watched him closely and critically. Her diary for 25 July 1894 records: 'Shaw lives in a drama or comedy of which he himself is the hero – his *amour propre* is satisfied by the jealousy and restless devotion of half a dozen women, all cordially hating each other.'

Influenced by William Archer, who remained a close friend despite the failed collaboration on the play, Shaw managed to find time to include play-going among his other activities. Archer was a strong defender of Ibsen, who was a controversial figure, regarded by many as a destroyer of social values. In 1890 Shaw drafted a lecture to the Fabians on the work of Ibsen, a congenial figure because of his social realism and strong views on freedom of thought and belief. *The Quintessence of Ibsenism* was published in an enlarged version in 1891, and the concentrated examination of plays such as 'The Wild Duck' and 'Brand' undoubtedly also concentrated Shaw's mind on the function and value of drama in disseminating ideas and changing people's perceptions of themselves and of the world. It was Shaw's most influential work so far.

In January 1891, Ibsen's 'A Doll's House' was produced in London, followed in February by 'Rosmersholm'. They were accorded far from classic status. To the conventional mind they were outrageous, subversive and thoroughly immoral. It was a familiar situation, as Shaw did not fail to point out in his essay:

'When the true prophet speaks, he is proved to be both rascal and idiot, not by those who have never read of how foolishly such learned demonstrations have come off in the past, but by those who themselves have written volumes on the crucifixions, the burning, the stonings, the headings and hangings, the Siberia transportations, the calumny and ostracism which have been the lot of the pioneer as well as of the camp follower.'

The Siberia transportations were of course those of Tsarist Russia, which writers like Dostoievsky had undergone. The Communist Shaw had no premonition of the Gulags to come.

As with earlier pioneers, Ibsen had his little band of faithful supporters, people who were wedded not just to him in a doctrinal sense, but who were advocates of a new approach in other arts as well. One of these was J. T. Grein, a tea merchant in the City of London. Grein had seen and been impressed by the avant-garde Théâtre Libre in Paris, and was prepared to support a similar venture in London, which began as The Independent Theatre. It had no hall of its own, and like Yeats's Irish Literary Theatre, which developed at the same time in Dublin, rented halls on a short term basis for its performances. The first production, in March 1891, was 'Ghosts'. It raised a tremendous storm, denounced as 'an open drain' and 'literally carrion', and was defended with spirit by Shaw, Archer and others. Its chief crime, for the worthy, was the role played in its story by venereal disease. Grein himself was vilified by many. He was a Jew, and a strong anti-Semitic strain can be found in the attacks on him. It was not an edifying episode. But, as Shaw's Fabian colleague A. B. Walkley, drama critic of the *Star,* prophetically noted, it was 'an epoch-making document in connection with the history of the English stage'. It opened the way for plays that could examine social questions in a more frank way, and present them with greater realism, than before.

Grein, shaken but undaunted by the abuse that 'Ghosts' had provoked, was keen to find a home-grown English play that dealt realistically with social issues. His problem, he confided to Shaw, was finding a play that was good enough. Shaw offered to solve his problem by writing one himself. The play begun with Archer, then laid aside, was taken up again after a seven-year interval. He had completed two acts, and now wrote a third, giving the play the title 'Widowers' Houses'. It was performed by the Independent Theatre Company at the Royalty Theatre on December 9, 1892. The subtitle, 'An Original Didactic Realistic Play', marked it out, for those who kept up with new developments, as very much part of the 'new drama', just as 'experimental' was to do at a later date. It ran for only two performances, but received a great deal of critical attention. Nor was its brief run ignored by the public. Both houses were well-filled, and cheers and boos competed with each other.

Shaw's first play shows the effects of the seven-year gap in its writing. The booing was not for its disjointed construction and rather ineffective ending, however, but for its politics. The activities of slum landlords had not before been considered matter for drama. Dickens, in novels like *Little Dorrit* and *Oliver Twist,* had exposed social evils, but Dickens had accomplished that with so much else in the way of story-telling, character, entertainment, humour, that the pill could be digested more readily. And novels were one thing; the public stage was another. Also, Shaw had no time at all for sentimentality and romanticism. Although the play has both character and humour, there is a quite un-Dickensian starkness about his work. The reader of Dickens might think, 'Oh, how dreadful', in turning the page to see what happened next. The viewer of Shaw was meant to think: 'Something ought to be done', and leave the theatre keen to do something about it.

'Widowers' Houses' owes much to Shaw's personal experience. He had collected rents from slum properties, and had thought long and hard before rejecting the ethics of the estate agent. He drew also on his own life in forming his characters, especially that of Blanche Sartorius, the violent-tempered daughter of the main character. She was closely modelled on Jenny Patterson, who at that time was still deeply involved with Shaw.

Piquantly, not least because Jenny was in the first night audience, the part of Blanche was played, with gusto, by Florence Farr. Shaw had known Florence for some years now, ever since his early visits to Kelmscott House, and she was one of the constellation of girls with whom he had been 'philandering'. For Florence, embroidery was either a diversion or something to be done between acting engagements. She was a woman of the theatre. Four years younger than

Shaw, she had seen more of real life than he had, having been married (to an actor called Emery, who had decamped to America). Now, with Shaw's attention increasingly focused on the theatre, and with Florence (who had been Rebecca West in 'Rosmersholm' in February 1891) as one of the Ibsenites, his interest in her turned from something more like trifling into something very like love. He wrote:

'This is to certify that – You are my best and dearest love, the regenerator of my heart, the holiest joy of my soul, my treasure, my salvation, my rest, my reward, my darling youngest child, my secret glimpse of Heaven, my Angel of the Annunciation ... '

Florence was very different from Jenny, being good-tempered and easy-going. With her, an affair might easily drift into sexual relations and yet she did not have any of Jenny's stormy possessiveness. Shaw loved her all the more for the contrast. He had told her of his long relationship but made it clear to Florence that it was she whom he loved:

'Not for 40,000 such relations will I forego one 40,000th part of my relation with you. Every grain of cement she shakes from it falls like a block of granite on her own flimsy castle in the air ... '

Jenny Patterson became aware that she had a rival far more serious than Mrs Besant. She did not give up the struggle tamely. On February 4, 1893, she went to Florence Farr's house and burst in upon Shaw and Florence. A violently

79

abusive scene followed, and Shaw had to prevent Jenny from attacking her rival. His diary records that it took two hours to get her out of the house, and he had to take her back to Brompton Square, which they reached about one in the morning, and from which he did not get away until three. This was effectively the end. Jenny Patterson and Shaw met a few times more, but it was clear that not even a platonic thread joined them now. Mrs Patterson retained her friendship with Mrs Shaw; but when Shaw knew of her coming, he would go out of the house.

Florence, sensuous and easy-going, shared Shaw's passion for music, but she was also deeply interested in poetry and had a mystical side to her nature that was quite alien to Shaw. While sharing his political views, she was not a political activist. Even at the height of his ardour for her, she was still seeing other admirers, and as the jealous Shaw well knew, was quite happy to let them make love to her. He remarked to his biographer Hesketh Pearson:

'She said herself that if a man started love-making, she felt at once as if she was up on the stage and must act up to his acting.'

To Florence, Shaw seemed over-intense, and she also detected a coldness in him. In 1910 she wrote a little book, *Modern Woman: Her Intentions,* in which she said that women did not care for sex unless they are: 'animated with the ardour of love. Passion served up with cold sauce as in the Shaw-Barker school of sex revolts them.'

– the overt reference is to love as depicted in the plays of

Shaw, produced by Barker, but Florence, who unlike Shaw believed in the soul, appears to have found an emptiness behind his rhetoric. Shaw's passion for her gradually subsided, its demise aided by his eventual realisation that she was not, as he had once supposed, the ideal actress to portray his characters. Before long, an alternative talent would catch his eye, and hers. Florence would become the lover of W. B. Yeats. She and Shaw remained good friends, linked by their common interests and the memory of a bygone and aimable romance.

Having seen his first play completed and performed, he was keen to continue, and rapidly wrote his second, 'The Philanderer'. Philandering was a word he used about himself, and the hero of the play was modelled on himself. It also includes a scene based closely on that in which Jenny broke in on him and Florence. Although offered to the Independent Theatre, it was not performed until 1905, and does not have many merits. Shaw's biographer St John Ervine, a drama critic as well as playwright, called it his worst play, and Shaw, looking back on it, described it in a letter to Ellen Terry as: '. . . a combination of mechanical farce with realistic filth which quite disgusted me . . .'

His third play, much more serious in intention, also suffered from delayed performance. 'Mrs Warren's Profession' was banned by the Lord Chamberlain, part of whose function was to read and vet all plays intended for public performance, a role that was only terminated in the 1970s. The reason for the ban was not the subject-matter of prostitution and its attendant evils, with which the play is very much concerned, but the slender element of incest in its story.

Apart from two private performances in 1902, the play was not staged until 1925.

So far, if viewed objectively, his career as a dramatist seemed to have got off to a very modest start. But Shaw was far from disheartened. He felt that he was doing something new in drama, but also that he knew what he was doing, and that recognition would come.

In 1894 Florence Farr became the manager of a season of new plays put on at the Avenue Theatre, in Northumberland Avenue, London. The season was financed by a wealthy young woman with a strong interest in the contemporary theatre, Annie Horniman (a few years later she was the financial backer of Yeats's Abbey Theatre in Dublin). Florence asked Shaw if 'Widowers' Houses' could be revived for it, but Shaw seized the chance to have a new play produced, and wrote 'Arms and the Man' at great speed. The first night was very well received. In a famous episode of British drama, there was one solitary hiss among the cheers. Shaw, taking his bows on the stage, said: 'I quite agree with you, sir, but what are we two among so many?' The hisser had thought the play was a satire on the British army. Despite the cheers, the play was not a financial success, running for eleven weeks to very small audiences. But its critical reception was very good. Shaw's friend Archer, who had disliked 'Widowers' Houses', and felt it showed that Shaw had no gift as a playwright, was completely converted, calling it: '... one of the most amazing entertainments at present before the public', and praising its comedy. It confirmed that Shaw was indeed a playwright. American performance rights were bought, and though it did not become a big hit, it became one of the standard repertory pieces of its purchaser, Richard Mansfield, a popular actor in the USA.

In September 1894, Shaw became drama critic of *The Saturday Review,* a paper edited by Frank Harris, the Irish-born adventurer-journalist who would write a biography of Shaw in 1931. Harris's conception of journalism was sensationalist for its time, and he was hoping for some good knockabout stuff in the mode of Corno di Bassetto. Although for Shaw, now a playwright himself, the position was rather more exposed and delicate than music-criticism, he often obliged, though the tone of his reviewing was generally more subdued. Surprisingly perhaps, he found little to please him in Oscar Wilde's masterpiece, 'The Importance of Being Earnest'. But the play was supremely un-earnest, and Shaw was, for all his flippancy and pleasure in paradox, an earnest person at heart. Didactic realism, however, had no appeal for Wilde. The leading playwright of the time was Arthur Wing Pinero, who was only a year older than Shaw but whose plays had been performed since 1877, and who had scored a major success with the 'realistic tragedy' of 'The Second Mrs Tanqueray' in the previous year. In a deeply critical review of Pinero's 'The Notorious Mrs Ebbsmith', a play based on the story of Mrs Besant, Shaw felt obliged to own:

'I disliked the play so much that nothing would induce me to say anything good of it. And here let me warn the reader to carefully discount my opinion in view of the fact that I write plays myself, and that my school is in violent reaction against that of Mr Pinero. But my criticism has not, I hope, any other fault than the inevitable one of extreme unfairness.'

Shaw returned to this theme in the introduction to his collected theatre criticism, calling his work:

'... not a series of judgements aiming at impartiality, but a siege laid to the theatre of the XIXth Century by an author who had to cut his own way into it at the point of the pen, and throw some of its defenders into the moat.'

His fifth play, 'Candida', was quite unrevolutionary, an engaging comedy, which was taken by the Independent Theatre Company, but was played only in the provinces, with no London production until 1904. He went on in 1897 to write a short play about Napoleon Bonaparte, 'The Man of Destiny'. Shaw was enough of a man of the theatre to try to form his plays with particular leading men and ladies in mind, and this one was written for Richard Mansfield, who however was not impressed and turned it down. Shaw then offered it to the capital's leading actor-manager, Henry Irving. Irving's name alone was worth a great deal to any production. Shaw had a great respect for Irving's acting ability, but throughout his drama reviews there runs a sustained note of criticism of Irving because Shaw regarded him as insufficiently interested in what was new and innovative in drama, and too complacent to give a lead. Shaw also detested the way in which Irving cut and adapted classic plays to enhance his own roles. Irving had therefore no cause to feel friendly to Shaw, and the situation was complicated by the fact that Shaw was a vociferous supporter of Irving's longtime leading lady, Ellen Terry. His opinion of Terry's abilities was extremely high, and when he saw her acting minor parts in trivial plays which were no more than vehicles for Irving to show his own genius off cheaply, he had no hesitation in saying so. Furthermore, he and Ellen Terry had become confidants in a strange romance-by-mail which had begun in 1892 and went on for several years before either of them actually met and talked to each other. It was with some diffidence on both sides that 'The Man of Destiny' was offered to Irving, who dithered with it for a long time, and never actually produced it. Shaw had envisaged Ellen Terry as the 'Strange Lady' in the play, and wrote to her: 'This is not one of my great plays, you must know; it is only a display of my knowledge of stage tricks ... You would like my 'Candida' much better'.

Soon afterwards, Shaw damned himself in Irving's eyes by writing a review of his production of Shakespeare's 'Richard III' which managed to imply that Irving, in what was undoubtedly a poor performance, had been drunk. Irving and his associates were furious; Shaw wrote to dissociate himself from the suggestion, but in a somewhat truculent tone. Irving made a sarcastic answer. Ellen Terry, Irving's long-term colleague, and Shaw's more recent correspondent-friend, was distressed. Any thought Irving might have had of taking on the Napoleon play were abandoned. Meanwhile things had not been going well at the rehearsals of the latest Shaw play, 'You Never Can Tell'. After protests from some of the actors about its lack of good lines for them, especially exit lines, the production was abandoned. Another disaster happened when the actor whom Shaw had designated for his latest play, 'The Devil's Disciple', William Terriss, was murdered at the stage-door of his theatre. Shaw believed not

85

in Fate but in a creative and evolutionary Life-Force, but Fate seemed to believe enough in him to award him a succession of disheartening blows.

Apart from small-scale private performances, and the rare involvement of well-off 'angels' of progressive views, like Grein and Annie Horniman, the professional London theatre was formed around a small number of actors. The number of theatres was limited; many were used only as music-halls. There was no National Theatre, and there were no state subsidies. Audiences, except for the very small number of real theatre enthusiasts, were attracted by the big names. Apart from Irving himself, and Ellen Terry, the other big star of the time was Stella Campbell, always known as Mrs Patrick Campbell (her husband was later killed in the Boer War). For Shaw, who with characters like Vivie in 'Mrs Warren's Profession', and Candida, and with others emerging in his thoughts, had 'New Women' very much in mind, the right leading lady was crucially important. There was therefore much reason for Shaw to take an interest in actresses. His stage woman did not 'know her place' as women in the male-dominated society of the time were normally expected to do. With a great respect for the female sex, which he believed to be in important respects more useful and creative than the male, he was determined to present women in commanding roles, and needed to feel that he had understanding friends among the leading ladies of the theatre, who knew what he was about, and who could play his strong-opinioned exemplar-women without the sentimentality and feminine deference that characterised most modern female parts, but whose talent for comedy could preserve their humour and prevent them from being strident. Of course, actresses were also attractive, even beautiful women, often warm-natured and always emotionally responsive to the hot-house atmosphere generated by a play in preparation, in which the playwright was a crucial figure. They were the ideal sort for Shaw's flirtatious approach to the female sex.

Better news came to Shaw in October 1897. Richard Mansfield's American production of 'The Devil's Disciple', with its War of Independence setting, which Shaw had finished that year, was very successful and soon handsome royalty payments were crossing the Atlantic. Jubilantly Shaw wrote to Ellen Terry: 'I roll in gold. I am a man of wealth and consideration. I will take a theatre presently, and engage Henry for eccentric comedy' (this last was a dig at Irving, the great tragic actor).

CHAPTER VI

A MARRIED MAN

Despite having a New York success, the episode with Irving, which ended with Irving resolved never to take anything written by Shaw, left Shaw in a state of temporary discouragement about his prospects as a playwright. The drama was still only one dimension of his life. He was still very much a politician and journalist. Fabian meetings, talks to Socialist and Communist gatherings, long discussions with people like the Webbs, whose preoccupation with politics was almost total (Beatrice Webb at this time regarded Shaw's playwriting as another example of his frivolity), all took up a great deal of his time. He was now earning a respectable income from journalism – the days of his poverty and penny-counting were past. To pursue a political-journalistic career seemed a perfectly good option, with the ultimate aim of a seat in Parliament. MPs at this time received no salary. A working man elected to Parliament needed the financial support of a trade union, unless he was able to become a journalist and maintain an income of his own. In what may have been a first step in this direction, Shaw moved from theoretical to practical politics by becoming a 'vestryman' of his local district of London, St Pancras. Before the reform of

London local government and the creation of the London boroughs and the London County Council, these local vestries administered district affairs. Shaw was co-opted into a vacancy on the vestry, without having to stand for election. He was still living with his mother in Fitzroy Square. His biographer R. F. Rattray notes that:

'He served on the Public Health, Parliamentary, Electricity, Housing and Drainage Committees. He fought the slum landlords and brothel keepers ... He was a pioneer in providing public lavatories for women. It was a difficult campaign. Councillors were shocked when Shaw suggested that some women should be members of the committee concerned.'

Although Shaw was capable of being a constructive and effective committee-man, as his Fabian work had already proved, there were clearly moments when his verve and relish for not only thinking, but speaking the unthinkable, was disconcerting for his fellow-councillors.

In the summer of 1896 he went to stay for six weeks with Sidney and Beatrice Webb, at a country rectory in Suffolk which they had taken for the summer. This was an annual event, enabling them to invite a range of guests and engage in political and social discussions and plan for the day when their ideas might be put into practice: very much part of the Fabian policy of 'permeation' of opinion-forming elements of society. These 'workshops' naturally also functioned as nests of gossip and personal intrigue. Beatrice Webb herself made a speciality of pairing off likely couples. Late in 1895 she had met a wealthy Irishwoman with left-wing leanings,

Charlotte Payne-Townshend, and speedily recruited her to the Fabian Society. Charlotte Payne-Townshend and Beatrice Webb became friends, and Charlotte joined the Rectory gathering as a joint tenant. As the surname suggests, she was a distant relative of the Townshend family who had been Shaw's first employers. Charlotte and Shaw became close friends, and Beatrice Webb, who had earmarked Charlotte for matrimony to a more tractable member of her circle, Graham Wallas, observed with some bemusement the development of romance between her new friend and the 'sprite' G. B. S. (By now he was firmly G. B. S. to all who knew him; of his two other names, he preferred Bernard to George; indeed he disliked George intensely; but his personal letters were all signed with his initials, which eventually became a sort of trademark.) Back in London, Shaw and Charlotte continued to meet, and she began to do secretarial tasks for him. He was already reflecting on the possibility of marriage, writing to Ellen Terry:

'… shall I marry my Irish millionairess? … I think I could prevail on her; and then I should have ever so many hundreds a month for nothing. Would you ever in your secret soul forgive me, even though I am really fond of her and she of me? No: you wouldn't.'

This kind of half-interior dialogue went on for some time. Shaw was in a very different situation from the May Morris one; he was already a well-known figure, at least in Labour politics and the London stage, and no longer hampered by the thought of poverty. But also his relationship with Charlotte Payne–Townshend was of a different kind to his previous dalliances. She was an independent woman, only six months younger than he was; they would both celebrate their fortieth birthdays in 1896. Shaw's energy and vivacity appealed to her; she saw beyond the brash exterior to his uncertainty, and his half-despairing urge to be loved. Their Irish background was something important that they shared: despite remaining firmly resident in England, neither of them ceased to feel essentially Irish, and to look upon the English as a friendly, kindred, but definitely different species to themselves. They felt at ease with each other, and Shaw's tendency to show off, to advance only one side of himself, was modulated by Charlotte's calm, though she was not always calm and Beatrice Webb at an early date noticed 'certain volcanic tendencies'.

When he met Charlotte, Shaw's affair with Florence Farr was not yet over. He was in full epistolary union with Ellen Terry, and he was frequently seeing Janet Achurch. His life was very much centred on London. Charlotte enjoyed travelling and hotels; she had become used to a life of relative leisure, whereas he was, and would remain, a workaholic who never liked to be far away from pen and paper. Although she was very much attracted to Shaw, she did not want to 'mother' him. Indeed she was distinctly averse to the notion of motherhood and children. She was happy to contemplate an intellectual and social partnership, and to manage a household where the cooking and cleaning would be undertaken by domestic staff. Marriage for both of them was desirable as a social partnership, but it might not have happened but for an accident to Shaw. By the end of 1896, their relationship was close and their feelings for each other were clear. But nothing came of it throughout 1897. Both had reasons for wariness. Shaw's 'philandering' was well-known to the Fabian circle and he showed no sign of giving up his friendships, though Florence ceased to be his mistress. Charlotte, who had been in love with the Swedish doctor and writer Axel Munthe, had a crucial reservation about marriage. She had acquired a revulsion for sexual activity and insisted that her marriage must be a chaste one. Despite the many speculations, from Frank Harris onwards, that Shaw was a man with a relatively weak sex drive, this must have appeared a major impediment. Nor was Charlotte offering the kind of open marriage that was not unknown in their progessive circle, in which husband and wife permitted each other sexual freedom. She would be fiercely and aggressively jealous of Shaw's relationships with other women.

Shaw led a healthy life in many ways, with his special hygienic clothing, and his enjoyment of walking, cycling and swimming. But in April 1898 he became ill. An injury to his foot, started by the habit of lacing up his shoes too tightly, turned into necrosis of the bone, a serious condition which might have required amputation. In addition he was very much run down through overwork, late nights and perhaps lack of regular nourishment. Charlotte Payne-Townshend had left the previous month to go with the Webbs on a world tour. Shaw's injured foot required surgery and he was obliged to go about on crutches. Mrs Shaw, by then aged sixty-eight, and never a particularly attentive mother, was of little help. Whether summoned by Shaw or by her own imperative, Charlotte heard about his condition and broke off her travels to return from Rome to London. Horrified by the squalor of Shaw's room in his mother's house, she insisted that he should be moved to her own house, and be looked after there. Shaw, however, said if he were to move under her roof, it must be as her husband. On June 1, 1898, they were married in the Strand District Registry Office, in London. They had Ellen Terry's blessing:

'How splendid! What intrepidity to make such a courageous bid for happiness. Into it you both go! Eyes wide open! An example to the world, and may all the gods have you in their keeping.'

Shaw had confided enough about some of Charlotte's reservations for his friend Ellen to believe that the gods would have some work to do.

The families on either side were not greatly pleased. Charlotte's sister felt that Shaw had married for the money; Shaw's sister Lucy, divorced from her own husband, was frankly jealous of their wealth, and referred to her brother's rich wife as 'the gall in our cup'. The despised 'Sonny' was winning all the prizes in life to which she herself had aspired in vain. Shaw was soon to win round his sister-in-law, but there was never any warmth between his wife and the Shaw women. Shaw himself remained on friendly if not close terms with Lucy, helping to maintain her home in Denmark Hill, south London, which he occasionally found a useful meeting-place for encounters of which Charlotte would have disapproved.

Although Shaw had failed as a novelist, he was, paradoxically, to become one of the most widely read authors in the world. Many thousands of people who never went to the theatre would read his plays. In this they were helped by his long, informative and entertaining prefaces, and by his extremely detailed stage directions, which not only give a description of the stage set and a physical description of the characters, and closely prescribe their movements and gestures, but also often explain what is going on inside their heads, and even what happens to them after the play is over. The reader's imagination is greatly assisted in envisaging the play taking place, putting the dialogue in its context. To read a Shaw play is an experience not unlike that of reading a novel, and, quite apart from performance royalties, with the royalties from huge international sales of popular editions, special editions, and promotional editions of his works, Shaw was able to enjoy a long and lucrative revenge over the art of fiction-writing.

The first two collected volumes appeared in the spring of 1898, under the titles *Plays Pleasant* (the comedies 'Arms and the Man', 'Candida', 'You Never Can Tell' and 'The Man of Destiny') and *Plays Unpleasant* ('Widowers' Houses', 'The Philanderer' and 'Mrs Warren's Professsion'). The reviews were as mixed as they had been for the plays, even William Archer, one of Shaw's two closest friends (the other being Sidney Webb) pulling no punches in his castigation of 'The Philanderer', whilst acknowledging 'Candida' as a work of genius. Meanwhile Shaw, convalescing in Surrey, where Charlotte had rented a comfortable house, was busy writing a new play, 'Caesar and Cleopatra'. Here he was quite consciously setting himself up against the greatest of all targets, the national bard of England himself, William Shakespeare. Shakespeare had written 'Antony and Cleopatra', a play of sultry magnificence, and 'Julius Caesar', a tragedy of false choices in statecraft. Shaw was not daunted. With what his detractors saw as colossal impudence, and what we might nowadays see as the writer 'psyching himself up', he made such pronouncements as these, for an in interview in *The Academy*:

'For years I was supposed to be brilliant and sparkling and audacious. That was quite a mistake. I am really slow, industrious, painstaking, timid. Only I have been continually forced into positions that I am bound to accept and go through with. I am not clever at all ... I am a genius. After all, I have accomplished something. I have made Shakespeare popular by knocking him off his pedestal and kicking him around the place, and making people realise that he's not a demi-god, but a dramatist.'

Having abandoned all hopes of Irving, Shaw wrote his play of Caesar with another vogue actor in mind, Johnston Forbes Robinson, as a leading man who could combine grandeur of character with a human lightness of touch. Shaw wanted a great man but also a credible one, and put a great deal of himself into the part. His Caesar is a man in whom the power of will is paramount, as was the case with the author. For Cleopatra ('she is an animal – a bad lot' he wrote to Ellen Terry, who would have liked the part herself), he wanted Mrs Patrick Campbell, and the essential first one-off performance, to establish the author's copyright, took place in Newcastle, with Mrs Campbell reading the part. But the play was not properly produced until 1907, with Robertson and Gertrude Elliott.

Shaw went on to write 'Captain Brassbound's Conversion', this time with Ellen Terry in mind as the heroine, Lady Cicely Waynflete. But to Shaw's consternation, she disliked the play and the part, and refused it, right up to the point when, reading it out in the copyright performance in Liverpool – she was about to leave for a US tour with Irving – she came round to like the play. But apart from a limited production by the Stage Society in 1900, it was not actually produced in London until 1906. Shaw's resourcefulness in getting his plays published meant that the play was, however, read by many people before it was seen on the stage. In 1898 he returned to the subject of music in a short work, *The Perfect Wagnerite*. Since his Dublin days he had been a supporter of Wagner, a composer who had as many denigrators as admirers. In this book he read a contemporary political significance into the complex allegory of Wagner's *Ring* cycle, seeing it as a metaphorical form of his own belief in Communism, with its ultimate withering away of social structures into a world of brotherly love. But, rather than being accomplished through Fabian gradualism, Shaw began to think in terms of heroes, individuals like his own Caesar, whose vision and steadfastness could change the world.

This intense writing activity and the attendant business negotiations took place whilst Shaw was still officially an invalid. For eighteen months in 1898–99 he was in a wheelchair or on crutches. The bone trouble in his foot lingered on for a long time, causing him acute distress at times, until he actually asked to have one of his toes amputated. But the surgeon refused, and the foot healed. Shortly after his marriage, he fell downstairs on his crutches and broke his arm. In the late summer he tried bicycling again, fell off, and sprained his ankle. This series of accidents had the effect of establishing the marriage on the basis on which it was to remain. Shaw's injuries and their attendant discomforts would have made a physical relationship difficult or impossible in any case. Instead, Charlotte fussed and managed and ensured he was properly nursed and cared for to the maximum extent that he would tolerate. This period of disability was a crux in Shaw's own view of his life. He felt it was a time when he might have died (septicaemia must have been a constant danger from his foot), and that in some sense he had passed through a form of death. But such deaths are merely the prelude to rebirth, and he sprang up from it with renewed physical vigour as well as creative energy. Every man of forty should have a year off to reconsider his life-direction, he announced. But he was from now on to be constantly aware of the enervating danger of a wealthy style of life. He could have lived in ease and comfort without earning another penny or writing another line. The thought was of course anathema to him. But now his daily life and his work became two separate apects of his existence, which had not been the case before his marriage. In mid-1899, by which time he had completed 'Captain Brassbound's Conversion' in about six months, he was taken on holiday, first to Cornwall, then on a Mediterranean cruise, which he thoroughly disliked. Returned to London, he moved into Charlotte's flat in

Adelphi Terrace, leasing his mother's house for her; she was joined there by her half-sister Arabella Gillmore and Arabella's niece. Lucy remained close to her ex-husband's family in Denmark Hill. Charlotte and Shaw returned to their rented Surrey house for long weekends. At that time it was common for accommodation to be rented on a long-term basis; and, because of Charlotte's enthusiasm for hotel life, they often stayed away.

In October 1899, while the Shaws were still cruising, the Boer War began. For the majority of English people and their politicians, this was an excuse to indulge in a fit of the crude imperialism that became known as 'Jingoism'. Those who, on the left of politics, disliked the war, the attitudes it aroused, and the way it was waged, were a minority. An anti-war Liberal MP was burned in effigy in his constituency. For the Fabian Society it was a difficult issue, yet one on which they felt they should give a lead. There was much discussion and the membership, of some 800, was polled to try to ascertain the Society's view; it merely showed the Society was heavily divided, with a small majority on the pro-War side. A number of pacifists and left-wing thinkers resigned from the Society. A new executive committee commissioned *Fabianism and the Empire,* described as being edited by George Bernard Shaw, though he largely wrote it, incorporating the comments of 134 other members. Shaw, an Irishman who wholly accepted the necessity of the United Kingdom, believed that the dominance in world affairs of the 'Great Powers' was a fact which should be accepted without question, though he expressed it as 'International Collectivism'. Sharing the Liberal unease about the ethics of imperialism, he was possibly the first writer to propose the British 'Commonwealth of Nations', though his version was somewhat more full-blooded as an institution than the post-imperial actuality. Shaw's generality of vision shows through clearly; he not only accepted the inevitability of the Great Power behaving as international policeman and trader as it pleased, able to impose on, even invade, a country which wanted to ignore the tide of history; he positively encouraged it. The tenor of his manifesto was thus that the Boer War was a just and necessary one. It was a controversial view, but it was expressed in terms that pleaded for Fabians to remain united and stick to their pragmatic view of political possibilities. It pleased Beatrice Webb, and displeased Shaw's own wife, who was a pacifist, but the manifesto had very little public impact.

Shaw, whose own writing is full of violence expressed in strong figures of speech, had on a rational level a deep hatred of war and violence, especially of unreasoning violence or violence against the helpless. But his view of his fellow-men was rather derogatory in this respect. He wrote:

'The Boer and the Britisher are both fighting animals ... Two dogs are fighting for a bone thrown before them by Mrs Nature ... The Socialist has only to consider which dog to back; that is, which dog will do most for Socialism if it wins.'

– a difficult point to resolve ... He was a lifetime boxing fan, it may be remembered; and came to enjoy the sport before the codification of the Queensberry Rules, when it was a bloodier business. He did not conceal it, and it was not an interest that he particularly sought to publicise, though in his novel *Cashel Byron's Profession,* the eponymous hero is a prize-fighter, and its dramatised version, the blank verse burlesque of Shakespeare 'The Admirable Bashville', of 1901, puts the boxer's case:

> '... this hand
> That many a two-days' bruise hath ruthless given,
> Hath kept no dungeon locked for twenty years,
> Hath slain no sentient creature for my sport.'

It was in 1900, at the copyright performance of 'Captain Brassbound's Conversion', that Shaw and Ellen Terry met face to face for the first time. The meeting was brief, and, as they had both feared might happen, it made a change to their paper relationship. Their exchange of letters, which at times reads more like those of actual lovers than of pen-friends, came to a halt for eighteen months before resuming again.

In November 1900 Shaw published his most recent texts in *Three Plays for Puritans.* The preface to the combined volume was a strong polemic against the way in which sex was treated and presented in contemporary theatre – his own New Drama excepted. He saw how preoccupied with sex the apparently genteel West End plays – and their audiences – really were; except that this 'systematic idolatry of sensuousness' was cloaked in ambiguity, in off-stage happenings, in a dishonest form of presentation that was 'as frankly pronographic as good manners allowed'. Shaw believed that this sub-erotic current had become like a drug that had managers and public hooked alike, and this 'habit' formed an almost insuperable obstacle to his own efforts to introduce a drama that was realistic and honest about events and human relationships. In his multi-volume biography of Shaw, Michael Holroyd notes that Shaw 'passes almost unnoticeably from demolishing the genteel assumptions of the sex-instinct as shown on the stage, to a demolition of the sex-instinct itself'. Holroyd sees Shaw, denied male gratification in his sexless marriage, as achieving his own potency by having his plays performed; without this accomplishment he is doubly impotent, and rages here against the sex-urge which is repressed in his own life, and which in its semi-repressed stage form also prevents him from justification by public success.

CHAPTER VII

A HOUSEHOLD NAME

'The Admirable Bashville', written in a week, was written partly because Shaw had heard that an unauthorised dramatic adaptation of his novel *Cashel Byron's Profession* had been performed in the USA. There was a great deal of fun in the play, though Shaw's efforts to render blank verse, even as a burlesque of the Shakespearean manner, do not make easy reading. Shaw already had a more substantial work on the stocks, referred to by him as 'an immense play, but not for the stage of this generation'. This was 'Man and Superman', with which he was to struggle until well into 1903. Its subtitle was 'A Comedy and a Philosophy', and it incorporated a Socratic-style debate, set in Hell, between Don Juan and the Devil, interpolated as a separate act into what otherwise was a three-act comedy. Its length and structure made him realise it was not – in this form – a play for the theatre, and he brought it out in book form in August 1903. His previous play collections had been published by Grant Richards, an enterprising and lively, though not very business-like publisher who became a friend. However, Shaw wanted to be his own publisher; himself arranging for setting and printing, and taking on the commercial risk, and employing a publishing company merely as his agent, to undertake the sales and distribution. He came to such an arrangement with Constable & Co., and his books were published in this way from then on. This system enabled Shaw to make greater profits, so long as the editions sold well enough. It also enabled him to put into practice a few ideas of his own regarding spelling and pronunciation. Elements of Shavian typographic practice, which he hoped would be followed by others, included ignoring the apostrophes in words like don't and can't, spelling 'haven't' as 'havnt', and simplifying spellings in the American manner, changing 'harbour' to 'harbor'. Whilst these disconcerted some readers, they were not obtrusive enough to be a deterrent. Regarded as quaint or eccentric usages rather than sensible or modernistic, they did not catch on with other writers, though some of Shaw's correspondents politely used them when writing to him. 'Man and Superman' is now seen as one of Shaw's greatest plays, a milestone in theatre as the first really successful philosophic play or play of ideas; but his friend William Archer, reviewing it in the *Morning Leader,* felt that Shaw had not done justice to his talent, and wrote to reproach him that he had 'done nothing really big, nothing original, solid, first-rate, enduring'. A sharper and more detached critic, Max Beerbohm, considered it Shaw's best work yet, praising especially his dialogue: 'In swiftness, tenseness and lucidity of dialogue no living writer can touch the hem of Mr Shaw's garment.' Beerbohm ascribed the brilliance of Shaw's dialogue to the fact that Shaw had perfected himself as an orator before he had done so as a writer. But he was critical of Shaw's character-drawing in the play (a view he handsomely recanted when the play was eventually performed on stage in 1905).

The Shaws' married life settled into a pattern of sorts, on the lines established in 1899. Charlotte Shaw, conscious of her role as the sustainer and protector of a great man, kept a vigilant eye on Shaw's working hours, and insisted on a regular change of scene. Their holiday travels took them to Italian hotels, Scottish lodges, English country houses, insanitary resorts visited by cruise liners – the protesting but obedient Shaw accompanying his wife, who promised him at each place that the next one would be better. Travel for its own sake did not appeal to Shaw in the least, and visits to such legendary places as Constantinople and the Greek islands did not produce any great mental stimulus, compared for example with the profound effect that the Ravenna mosaics had on W. B. Yeats and his work, a few years later. Shaw's inspiration was not a mystical past but the problems and attitudes of an all-too-real, and often thoroughly unpleasant, present, with which his active, critical and constructively minded brain maintained a constant dialectic.

Although through the conservatism of managers and actors, and occasional acts of Fate, his dramas were still largely unperformed on the English stage, Shaw's reputation, already higher in the USA than in England, was also beginning to spread in Europe. In 1902, through William Archer, he had been introduced to an unworldly seeming young Austrian writer, Siegfried Trebitsch, who despite a limited command of English had become a fervent admirer of Shaw's work. With some reluctance, Shaw allowed Trebitsch to acquire German-language production rights, and to undertake German translations of his first ten plays. In February 1903 'The Devil's Disciple', in Trebitsch's version, was performed at the Raimund Theatre in Vienna. Other Austrian and German productions followed, and gained Shaw a high reputation as a dramatist, perhaps the first English-language playwright since Shakespeare to be really esteemed in the German-speaking countries.

Shaw's involvement in local politics came to an end when in Spring 1904 he had to stand for election as a borough councillor for St Pancras South. He took the label of Progressive Party candidate, and campaigned robustly but with full play given to that lack of seriousness which sensible friends of his so deplored. He paraded his Communism, atheism and teetotalism, spouted paradoxes and intelligent witticisms that were wasted on the smoky air, and came an utterly unabashed third. Whilst he maintained his close involvement with the Fabians, and continued to lecture up and down the country, he did not venture again into the electoral arena. He commented that it was better to send his ideas, rather than himself, to the House of Commons.

At the same time, his fortunes on the London stage were about to change. In April 1904 'Candida' was put on at the Royal Court Theatre in Sloane Square, on the outer fringe of London's West End. Its director was Harley Granville-Barker, its business manager the theatre's manager, John E. Vedrenne. The run was successful enough for the duo to attempt a more ambitious season in the autumn of 1904, in the same theatre. 'Candida' was in the repertoire, together with a new play by Shaw, and other plays, in what was a distinctly avant-garde programme including a version of

Euripides' 'Hippolytus' by Gilbert Murray, and a translated version of 'Aglavaine and Selysette' by the Belgian symbolist playwright Maurice Maeterlinck.

Shaw's range of acquaintance in London's political, literary and dramatic worlds was now a very wide one. It was also rising up the social scale. As the Fabian Society gained numbers and influence (and the Webbs in particular worked very hard to gain friends and converts in high places) so leading politicans began to respond to their concerns and plans; chiefly on the Liberal side, but radically minded Conservatives too were interested. Shaw had known Harley Granville-Barker since 1900, when he had seen him act the part of Marchbanks in the Stage Society's production of 'Candida'. Barker had ambitions as a playwright and director; Shaw developed a deep respect for the younger man's talents – he was twenty-one years younger – which resulted in a close friendship for many years. Shaw had in many ways been ahead of his time. It was Barker who would successfully present Shaw's plays to his own generation.

The new Shaw play for the Royal Court season was 'John Bull's Other Island'. This play had been requested by W. B. Yeats, who had formed the Irish Literary Theatre Company in Dublin. In December 1904 this would take permanent form as the Abbey Theatre company. Yeats had watched the growth of Shaw's dramatic career and wanted from him an 'Irish' play. The request was made at a time when Shaw was feeling disenchanted with the London stage and his inability to cut his way through its conservatism. He had not been back to Ireland since he had left it nearly thirty years before. His personal experience of his native land was therefore seriously out of date; on the other hand his contact with other Irish writers, such as Yeats, Lady Gregory, and Moore, and his voracious reading of the daily newspapers, meant that he was quite up to date with much that was going on there. Working at furious speed through 1904, since the play was wanted for the Abbey's opening season, he sent it to Yeats at the end of September. But Yeats and his associates stalled; Yeats himself did not care for the play, despite recognising many of its great qualities. After much hedging and prevarication, the Abbey finally gave up its option on the play (it eventually did produce it, but not till 1916). The way was open for the Royal Court to take it, and Shaw worked hard to cut its considerable length, worked hard again with the actors in rehearsal, and it was performed on November 1, 1904. It was a success from the start. Beatrice Webb brought the Prime Minister, Arthur Balfour (a Conservative) to see it, and he returned a further four times. The final accolade was delivered when in March 1905 a special performance was put on for the King, Edward VII. He found it so entertaining that he fell out of his chair. Shaw, the unperformed author of unpopular plays, was suddenly a celebrity playwright, and the middle England which had happily ignored him, began to feel instead that a treat might be in store.

The play in book form was Shaw's first best-seller, going through five impressions in two years. With a typical form of reaction, Shaw, who had struggled for years to achieve success and recognition as a playwright, began to feel that it was the wrong sort of success. The play, he thought, had been too easy, too shallow; the laughs had not been thought-provoking.

107

He had set out out to prick at the English Liberal view of
Ireland, and had discovered that the English are entirely capable of laughing at themselves without wishing to do a
thing about making themselves different. His response was
to embark almost at once on a new play, that would make
them pay attention.

He wrote it with a new leading actress in mind, Eleanor
Robson, who had become famous in more conventional
dramas. Shaw had hoped she would play Gloria in a production of 'You Never Can Tell', but the actress felt that the play
was too much of a 'freak' one. Having created a saintly figure
in the person of Father Keegan in 'John Bull's Other Island',
Shaw wrote to Eleanor Robson to say he wanted to see if he
could make a woman saint too. The resulting play was 'Major
Barbara', in which the heroine is a Salvation Army officer.
Shaw had always had a soft spot for the Salvation Army, for
its music and its charitable concern for the urban poor
rather than its theology. The persona he installed into the
Salvationist uniform was chiefly that of Beatrice Webb, a
woman of spiritual qualities, of steely will, of action, but also
capable of charm. Bombarded by requests for new productions, and with the Royal Court team busy on a series of re-
vivals of his earlier plays, Shaw was becoming quite exhausted. He found time to dash off a short 'tomfoolery', 'Passion, Poison and Petrification', for the Actors' Orphanage. In
the summer of 1905 Charlotte took him for a prolonged stay
in Ireland. They stayed in the County Cork house that had
been her childhood home, Derry House, near Rosscarberry,
and here Shaw continued to work on the new play. 'Major
Barbara' tackles head-on the issue of wealth and poverty, its

main theme, described by Shaw as 'the way of life lies through the factory of death', driven by Shaw's knowledge that millions of people in Britain, then at its imperial peak, lived unfulfilled lives in poverty and often degradation in the towns and cities. As the ultimate symbol of the capitalist world, he took the arms industry, already a vast global industry, in which 'Major Barbara's' father, Undershaft, has made his millions by selling arms to whoever was able to pay. Another person characterised in the play, and much consulted in the latter stages of its writing, was Gilbert Murray, an Australian assimilated into the British academic establishment as Professor of Greek at Oxford, and into the social establishment by an aristocratic marriage, but who remained an independent, idealistic democratic anarchist, a friend of Bertrand Russell and John Buchan as well as of Shaw.

Vedrenne and Granville Barker were an effective combination. The theatre manager was cautious, pessimistic, and very conscious of the budget. The director was determined to give the plays the kind of production that they needed in order to make their full impact. The new season from May 1905 confirmed the fact that Shaw was a box-office draw; two plays ran together on a daily basis, one in the matinee performance, the other in the evening. At the same time he was gaining immense publicity in the United States where Arnold Daly's production of 'Mrs Warren's Profession' was banned in New Haven and in New York. This was almost a routine hazard for non-conventional theatre companies: the Abbey players from Dublin had been arrested in Philadelphia for playing John M. Synge's 'The Playboy of the Western World'. When the case was brought to court, the judge

109

ruled in favour of the production, despite the ardent protests of the Society for the Suppression of Vice. The resultant notoriety did no harm when the actor Robert Loraine, after long perseverance, was finally able to produce 'Man and Superman' at the Hudson Theatre, New York, in September 1905. It was a great success (although the published version was banned from the city's Public Library). It could be said of the USA as well as of England that Shaw, as St John Ervine wrote: 'created an intelligent audience for intelligent plays and educated actors and actresses who could perform in them.'

Following 'Major Barbara' came another big 'play of ideas', 'The Doctor's Dilemma'. The Royal Court had become a Shavian centre, almost perhaps the family that Charlotte and Shaw did not have in the conventional parent-child sense. Both the Shaws took a quasi-parental interest in Granville Barker, and Shaw extended this interest to Lillah McCarthy, the actress who played Ann Whitefield in 'Man and Superman'. Barker and McCarthy married, to Shaw's dismay: 'there were no two people on earth less suited to one another'. In 'Man and Superman', Granville Barker, playing John Tanner, was got up to look like Shaw himself. For Lillah McCarthy, who regarded the playwright with veneration, it may have been as close as she could get to Shaw's own embrace. Contemplating his new play, he wrote to her that it: '. . . will be a complete success for you, for me, for the Court and for the Universe'. The Royal Court, at the height of the Barker-Vedrenne-Shaw collaboration, with all its success, and its ambition to lead to a British National Theatre, was far from being a harmonious enterprise. Argument, disagreement and angry disputes were part of its make-up. Part of the problem was the repertory system, which the Vedrenne-Barker partnership had basically introduced into the modern British theatre, with its requirement of change and variety and its demands on a small company ('flesh and blood cant stand the racket of it,' wrote Shaw). Part was also the theatrical temperament. The same aspects of personality that could catch fire in front of an audience and put life into Shaw's arguments, witticisms and paradoxes, could also blaze up in a dressing-room quarrel or at some parsimony by the management.

The target of the new play was one of the biggest bastions of complacency, power and narrow thinking – the medical profession. Shaw had made the acquaintance of a leading London doctor and medical researcher, Sir Almroth Wright, who had made what was believed to be a breakthrough in vaccination treatment, and had asked him the question: 'What would happen if more people applied to you for help than you could properly look after?' Wright's reply: 'We should have to consider which life was worth saving', gave Shaw the necessary idea (Shaw and Wright were to be rival debaters, each demolishing the other, only to see him rise again, for decades to come). Wright helped Shaw in the writing of 'The Doctor's Dilemma', though as Michael Holroyd points out, the true crux of the play is not whether the obnoxious but brilliant artist is worth more than the decent, humble doctor, but rather the process by which we arrive at judgements, and then justify those judgements both to ourselves and to others that gives the play its tension. Wright was not gratified by his depiction as Sir Colenso Ridgeon in the play.

111

Another source of the play's gestation was a challenge from Archer, still anxious for his friend Shaw to do something big. He had written an article, 'Death and Mr Shaw', suggesting that Shaw was incapable of writing a convincing death scene, being too impishly minded to establish a tragic sense. Shaw was far too intelligent to try to reproduce dead effects, and the death scene of the artist Dubedat, in its black comedy (Shaw said 'it will probably be called a "farce macabre"') anticipates much of later twentieth-century theatre. It was by no means well understood at the time: 'Amateurs of the morbid will revel in this realistic death-scene,' wrote *The Times*. The play had a somewhat mixed critical reception and was not, on its first production, the complete success that Shaw had prophesied, but it was brought back at the end of 1906, when it had a successful run.

As a successful playwright, Shaw could feel that he had established a platform far bigger than the soapboxes or platform podiums of his Socialist lectures, and was reaching a much wider constituency of listeners. But he continued to give talks, for no fee, charging only for his modest expenses in getting from place to place. The Fabian Society, in which he remained a powerful force, had been going through a difficult time. The Labour Party had emerged as a separate political force, established with the support of the trade unions. Whilst the Fabians might feel themselves its godparents, it did not acknowledge their role. The Fabian concept of permeation, of influencing the highly placed, was questioned by many members who felt that the Webbs were spending too much time entertaining aristocratic Liberal and Conservative politicans while the people's party was organising itself without the benefit of proper Fabian involvement. A leader in the reform movement of the Fabians was the writer H. G. Wells, who had become a member in 1903 and who in February 1906 produced a highly critical paper entitled 'Faults of the Fabians'. Wells's energy resulted in the setting-up of a committee to examine how the Fabian Society could increase its 'scope, influence, income and activity'. Wells wanted to turn the Fabian Society into a large movement, but was completely outmanoeuvred by Sidney Webb and Shaw, who recognised some justice in Wells's criticisms, but also realised that he would have completely wrecked the whole aim and ethos of the society. The discussions went on through the winter of 1906–7. Wells resigned as a Fabian in 1908, but he and Shaw remained friends, despite many disagreements and a sense on each side that he understood the other man perfectly, but that the other man did not understand him at all. There was a strong sense of rivalry between the two, which Shaw, for all his desire to placate Wells and keep him in the Society, did nothing to diminish, and some of their correspondence reads more like the exchanges of a pair of too-clever-by-half schoolboys than anything else. A long admonitory letter from Shaw to Wells at the height of the debate about the future of Fabianism comments:

'... I, thank heaven, am an ORATOR, and not a mulish draper's assistant ... Why is it that you can't write a play, and I can? You think it is because you don't choose. Yah!'

– the tone is deliberately rough and man-to-man; Shaw thought that this was the way to get through to Wells, but Wells wrote back in the same spirit to tell him his letter was bosh.

It was, however, typical of Shaw, as many of his friends and associates noted, that he could deliver scathing criticism without personal offence. He was also, usually, mild in his receipt of criticism, at least from those people whom he liked or respected. William Archer and A. B. Walkley frequently assailed him in reviews, but Shaw remained humorously imperturbable. Against their strictures, he could point to his success – the number of his plays in performance throughout the world, the editions of his work in print, the size of his royalty statements.

He felt free to write the plays he wanted to write. Now that public taste, at least among the intelligent theatre-goers, had caught up with him, he wanted to stay a step ahead. In 1908 appeared what he called a 'Disquisitory Play', 'Getting Married'. In this thoughtful comedy the institution of marriage in England is examined from many angles through a set of shifting relationships and attitudes. Not one of Shaw's major plays, it is still worthy of a closer look since it shows clearly how he set out to make his audience pay attention to his themes. One innovation is its lack of any interval: the play flows through a series of scenes with no natural break until its end. Although there is relatively little action, there are many surprises and dramatic situations. There are dramatic tensions between different characters. There is suspense. There is the rich additive of humour, and plenty of challenging remarks:

Edith: Of course I shall work when I'm married. I shall keep your house.

Sykes: Oh, that!

Reginald: You call that work?

Edith: Don't you? . . . Does your present housekeeper do it for nothing?

Reginald: But it will be part of your duty as a wife.

In the preface, almost as long as the play itself, Shaw addresses 'the evils of indissoluble marriage' which are entertainingly exposed in the play. At the time his own marriage was under some stress; a young woman called Erica Cotterill, a cousin of the poet Rupert Brooke, had become infatuated with Shaw. For several years she attempted to hurl herself against the rampart of the Shaw marriage, believing herself destined to be his true spiritual mate and also the mother of his children. Convinced by his mother's attitude, from an early stage in his life, that he was not a loveable person, Shaw was susceptible to such approaches, and also began to feel a sense of responsibility for his importunate admirer. Charlotte resented what she saw as his encouragement of an unbalanced woman, and in the end made him write a letter, which she signed, forbidding Erica any further contact.

As a further indication that Shaw was by no means allowing himself to become an establishment figure, or rest on his fame, his next two plays, both short ones, were banned by the Lord Chamberlain's department, one, 'Press Cuttings', because its leading characters were too obviously based on Lord Kitchener and Mr Asquith (Mitchener and Balsquith);

the other, 'The Shewing-Up of Blanco Posnet', because it referred to God in a disrespectful manner. 'Blanco Posnet' was put on at the Abbey Theatre in Dublin, as a gesture against censorship, since the Lord Chamberlain of England had no jurisdiction there. It was a great success, although played in a city where the resident Cardinal possessed equally keen heresy-detecting antennae to the Lord Chamberlain of England, and far greater popular authority. London critics came and commented on how 'Everyone today is enjoying the story of Mr Shaw's cleverness and the Censor's folly' (*The Times*). Other playwrights suffered the censor's ban, including Harley Granville Barker, but the banning of new works by the now-prominent Shaw had the effect of intensifying the already strong agitation in literary and political circles for a change in attitude, and a joint select committee of Parliament was established to look at the matter. Its conclusions, after hearing evidence from many leading writers and critics, apart from Shaw himself, led to some relaxation of theatre censorship, though not to its abolition. The affair allowed Shaw to indulge his high spirits to the full. He prepared a long statement to the committee, which the committee rejected, having been startled by its second paragraph:

'I am not an ordinary playwright in general practice. I am a specialist in immoral and heretical plays. My reputation has been gained by my persistent struggle to force the public to reconsider its morals. In particular, I regard much current morality as to economic and sexual relations as disastrously wrong; and I regard certain doctrines of the

Christian religion as understood today in England with abhorrence. I write plays with the deliberate object of converting the nation to my opinions in these matters.'

This was shocking, frightening stuff for most members of parliament in 1909. The whole statement is reproduced in the preface to 'The Shewing-Up of Blanco Posnet', or 'A Sermon in Crude Melodrama', set in the USA, a country of which Shaw had no direct knowledge; and its banning, as so often with works of art, made it far more famous than its own interest or qualities merited. It is questionable whether Shaw helped or hindered the censorship debate by such a tactic; but there is no doubt that he was serving his own wider purpose. It was by the public expression of such attitudes that his fame spread among people who took little interest either in theatre or in politics. Like little mines dug under a massive wall, they made a strong contribution to eventually toppling many of the official and unofficial restrictions of social life and opening the way to what was labelled 'the permissive society'. Shaw has been compared to Thomas Carlyle as a moral guide, though with different aims. The critic John Gross described Carlyle's immense influence as 'vague, a something-in-the-air rather than an ideology'; similarly, Shaw encouraged a change in social attitudes by asking questions, by saying the unthinkable, and by pointing out absurdities, anomalies and hypocrisies in social life.

CHAPTER VIII

𝒜 THOROUGHLY MODERN PLAYWRIGHT

One of the things that happened to Shaw, from the time of his fame onwards – and with his own enthusiastic participation – was that he became a popular icon. The image of the playwright-thinker, striking and distinctive as it was, with its long, strong face, centre-parted hair, sparkling eyes beneath bristly eyebrows, and jutting beard, the long body clad in its all-wool jacket, knickerbockers and stockings, was one that became instantly recognisable to the British and Irish public in a way that perhaps only monarchs could equal. A keen photographer (and self-photographer), Shaw posed happily for photo-portraits, portraits in oils, engravings and sculptures. Just about every portraitist of note, in the various media, had a go. Like Voltaire, he had no objection to being depicted nude. He was the subject of hundreds of drawings and caricatures, and was even to be found rendered into such objects as china statuettes and brass door-knockers. At Charlotte's instigation he travelled to Paris to sit for a bust by Auguste Rodin, the greatest sculptor of the day. The Austrian poet Rainer Maria Rilke, then working as Rodin's secretary, recorded how the Irish playwright put such energy into simply posing motionless that: 'he has the power of getting his whole self, even to his legs and all the rest of him, into his bust ...' It was an age of newly fledged mass-communication, and Shaw understood and embraced it; he had a shrewd instinct for the manipulation of the media, then a less sophisticated art than now; and used it cheerfully for his own propaganda purposes. It was not yet an era in which a person could be famous just for being famous. It was necessary to do things. Shaw did a great many things, and was adept at making them known. For all the self-deprecation that laces his writings, he was a vain man who relished his own celebrity. He wanted to be famous. The long years of unpaid obscurity had flowered at last and he made himself into a most exuberant blossom: 'good copy' for the pressmen looking for a quote; always ready to pose for the camera. He could make capital even out of failure. Fenner Brockway, a left-wing Socialist standing for Parliament in Lancaster in 1922, had Shaw come to speak for him: it was a flop.

'... he never got going and the audience was bored. He saved it by his last sentence. "Ladies and gentlemen," he declared, his voice vibrant at last, "you will be able to inform your incredulous grandchildren that you heard Bernard Shaw when he was dull." '

Brockway noted that Shaw was deeply ashamed, but his final remark was: 'I shall recover reading my own incomparable writing.' He spent the long journey home correcting his

119

latest set of proofs. The often brazen public flamboyance was far from being the whole extent of Shaw's personality. He showed only what he chose to show, and preserved his essential privacy. Many of his letters were destroyed by himself. Some of his best human qualities were hidden. Although he liked to depict himself as as a penny-pincher, he was in fact generous, and discreetly so. Many of his private acts of kindness emerged only with the publication of letters after his death.

Although Charlotte's Adelphi Terrace flat had always been a London base, they had been looking for a country house not too far from the capital. In November 1906 the series of rented homes was ended when the Shaws bought themselves a house at Ayot St Lawrence in Hertfordshire. This was a recent building (1902) but named 'The Rectory' as if it had been there from time immemorial; neither of them cared greatly for it and most of their friends thought it a commonplace and ugly, rather suburban, house. Despite frequent complaints about it, and announced intentions to find somewhere else, it was to be their home until the end. Shaw renamed it as 'Shaw's Corner', and it remains open to the public, as a memorial to him, in the care of the National Trust, still somewhat charmless. He did much of his writing in a specially built shed in the garden, also still preserved. Adelphi Terrace was retained, and both addresses were printed on the postcards which Shaw used for his terse communications, and his replies to the vast number of people who wrote to him. As time went on, the volume of his mail increased vastly. The postman of Ayot St Lawrence had good reason to regret the day the playwright-sage had moved in. Shaw was driven to keep a stock of pre-printed postcards with the most common responses to his mail-bag ready for sending off. From 1907 onwards he employed a secretary, the first being a relative of his own, who was staying with his mother at the time, Georgina Gillmore.

He worked unceasingly. On the train to Manchester, to deliver a lecture, he would write down a scene for his new play; waiting to be introduced to the audience, he would draft an article on votes for women or the evils of colonialism; he was never idle except when his wife insisted, as she frequently did, on his laying down his pen for a change of activity. Their travels continued, with Charlotte often taking him away to some rural retreat or foreign place where it was only with great difficulty that he could snatch time to continue writing. A new diversion was the Fabian summer school, a sort of residential camp where London Fabians met their country colleagues, participated in eurhythmic exercises, consumed vegetarian fare, listened to lectures by Shaw and other luminaries, and generally stocked up on high-mindedness for another year.

Left to his own devices, Shaw might have been happy to remain in London, with occasional outings, for political meetings, to large cities. Charlotte's impetus took him to Sweden, back again on several occasions to Ireland, as well as to Scotland, France, Switzerland, Germany and Italy. Most of the time they stayed in hotels, though in Ireland they often stayed with family friends of Charlotte's, members of the castle-dwelling Anglo-Irish ascendancy who looked somewhat nervously or suspiciously on her husband, the self-proclaimed Communist and wrecker of public morality, who had once been a cashier in an estate-office in Dublin. Shaw was not a man to be patronised, however; quite apart from remembering that the Shaws and Gurlys had had their own place in Irish history, he was fully conscious of his own worth and importance, and displayed this, not arrogantly but with a courtesy and charm that made the grandees feel that the privilege was theirs. At this time the issues of Irish cultural nationalism were being hammered out in debate and confrontation – and a memorable theatrical evening of riot – in Dublin, with Yeats and Synge defending their view of an English-language future against the Pearse-Hyde crusade for a Gaelic-speaking nation. The same sides were taken on the question of union against independence. These were not issues that engaged Shaw, though his sympathies, like those of most of the people with whom he stayed, undoubtedly lay with the English language and the British union. Sometimes the Shaws' travels provided an opportunity to meet another great spirit. In Stockholm, a meeting was arranged between Shaw and the Swedish dramatist August Strindberg, and a special performance of Strindberg's 'Miss Julie' was put on, in Swedish. Shaw appreciated the compliment and was pleased to meet Strindberg, for whose genius he had a sincere appreciation, but any real communication was very difficult. The meeting was eventually terminated by Strindberg, who took out his watch, observed, in German, that it was half past one and that at two o'clock he was going to be sick. But Shaw's admiration for Strindberg would bear fruit later, when he was awarded the Nobel Prize for

Literature, and donated the prize money to the Swedish drama community.

As befitted an apostle of modernism, Shaw was enthusiastic about the many new devices that technological development brought. He had long been a user of the telephone. At the end of 1908 he purchased a motor car, having already had a few driving lessons. A chauffeur-mechanic was also employed, but Shaw very often took the wheel himself. The car was an expensive one, a Lorraine-Dietrich, and Shaw by no means confined its use to country byways around Ayot St Lawrence. It was taken on adventurous tours to Algeria, to Ireland, to France. Shaw found in it a rich source of anecdote for letters and journalism. Others did too. His driver from 1919 onwards, Fred Day, recorded how Shaw was apt to put his foot on the accelerator when the brake was needed. Shaw also experimented with a motor bike at various times. When he was about fifty-five, Day recorded: 'He went out with her one day and I don't know what happened, but he came back and said, "The bike got me down and got on top of me. Someone pulled it off me, and I got up and came home." He didn't use it much after that.' Shaw also went up in a hot-air balloon with the actor and man-of-action Robert Loraine, and Charlotte's sister Mary in 1906, rising to 9,000 feet above London, before landing in the country in the field of a 'purple-faced individual'. Ten years later he flew in a three-seater aeroplane, on a demonstration flight which included looping the loop. The pilot observed that his passenger stood the display without turning a hair. From the 1930s on, Shaw, egalitarian though he was, owned a Rolls-Royce, the most conspicuously plutocratic car on the market.

Shaw had replaced God and the entire apparatus of religion with his concept of the evolutionary Life-Force. He was not a scientific or rationalistic atheist. In a sense he was not an atheist at all. Sending a copy of 'The Shewing-Up of Blanco Posnet' to the Russian writer Lev Tolstoy, he wrote:

'To me God does not yet exist; but there is a creative force constantly struggling to evolve an executive organ of godlike knowledge and power; that is, achieve omnipotence and omniscience, and every man and woman born is a fresh attempt to achieve this object ...'

– in this way Shaw was able, half-playfully, to account for evil in the world, saying of a disease bacillus that it 'was an early attempt to create a higher being than anything achieved before that time, and that the only way to remedy the mistake was to create a still higher being, part of whose work must be the destruction of that bacillus ...' Later he would put the bacillus itself on stage.

The Life-Force preserved considerable latitude for mystical and religious thought, and Shaw himself always found religion an irresistible subject. He found the society of religious people to be congenial to him, and this feeling was reciprocated. One of his closest friends was the author G. K. Chesterton, a fervent convert (in 1922) to Catholicism, of extremely fat physique, and a highly original writer and stylist whose sense of humour is akin to Shaw's in its delight in the paradoxical and topsy-turvy. As with Sir Almroth Wright, a debater-friendship began. Shaw and

Chesterton shared platforms, to the edification, entertainment and sometimes alarm of their audiences, the one denouncing religion as superstition, the other placidly agreeing about the paganism of the English but asking what that had to do with ultimate truth; the one preaching his idealised and extreme socialism, in which everyone would own everything and no-one would own anything; the other preaching the gospel of distributism – a wider spread of ownership of property. Both brilliant talkers with large and capacious minds and memories, both tall, commanding figures, though Chesterton's bulk was almost twice that of Shaw's, they defended opposite points of view with gusto and mutual cordiality. Both were deeply sincere and earnest men, who cloaked their earnestness in verbal fireworks and mental high spirits, and each felt the other did not quite grasp his essential seriousness: 'I wish I could persuade Mr Chesterton that I really am a serious man dealing with a serious question,' complained Shaw at one point. Laughter was always seen by Chesterton as a great weapon. He refused to take Shaw seriously. But the trend of popular thought was on Shaw's side. The country was growing steadily less religious in attitude and behaviour. It showed no sign of espousing the Life-Force, however. An intellectually undemanding materialism was emerging as the national credo.

Shaw the playwright turned his attention to a new subject in 1909, with a second 'disquisitory' play, 'Misalliance'. The topic was the relations of parents and children – something on which he felt deeply. His mother was still alive, aged nearly seventy, maintained by him in rather greater comfort than he had been maintained by her. The events of the play take place within a single day in one house. Shaw had read and been partly inspired by Granville Barker's play 'The Madras House'. As Shaw's biographer Michael Holroyd points out, it was a play much better understood a generation later, when its original features, 'these same qualities of unreality and madness, and the fracturing of standard plot procedures, have again altered their focus and may be seen as having their destination in the mystification and illusion of modern theatre.' In the preface to the play Shaw sets out his views on how custom and tradition set out to destroy exactly what in the child should be encouraged – its newness, its aspiration towards a further stage of the Life-Force which has produced it; and after a long diatribe against education, proposes the Juvenile Magna Carta or Declaration of Rights. He casts a cold eye upon the family:

'. . . though parents and children sometimes dislike one another, there is an experience of succor and a habit of dependence and expectation formed in infancy which naturally attached a child to its parent or to its nurse (a foster parent) in a quite peculiar way . . . there is no such impulse to suffer our sisters and brothers, our aunts and uncles, much less our cousins. If we could choose our relatives, we might, by selecting congenial ones, mitigate the repulsive effect of the obligation to like them and to admit them to our intimacy. But to have a person imposed on us as a brother merely because he happens to have the same parents is unbearable when, as may easily happen, he is the sort of person we should carefully avoid if he were anyone else's brother.'

Shaw, of course, had no brother. But he did grow up with two older sisters. There is a coldness and strength of feeling in this passage, and a lack of his typical wit, that seems to offer an insight not only into Shaw's abstract or intellectual view of the family, but his personal view.

The play was presented as part of a repertory season produced by the American Charles Frohman. Frohman had hoped that London was ready for a a regular programme of 'highbrow' theatre, put on professionally with top actors in a large West End theatre, the Duke of York's. In fact the effort was a failure. The audiences were not large enough. The confused and hostile public reaction to 'Misalliance', the second play to be presented, did not help. It seemed too strange, too full of talk, with no real action to take it anywhere. In the course of 1910 Shaw also produced three short plays, 'The Glimpse of Reality', 'The Fascinating Foundling', and 'The Dark Lady of the Sonnets'. The last was written to raise funds for the National Theatre project, another Shavian cause, which would not materialise until well after the playwright's death. Among Shaw's now very wide circle of friends, Sidney and Beatrice Webb continued to occupy a special place, along with a small number of other close friends like William Archer and Harley Granville Barker. Sidney and Beatrice, following the publication of a series of important books, had become influential people. He had been instrumental in creating the London School of Economics, a pioneer institution of its kind. She had served on the government's Poor Law Commission, filing a lengthy minority report. All of them were still senior members of the Fabian Society. Reconstituted and revived after the Wellsian attack, the Society was quite vibrant, though it had no generation of giants rising up to replace the founders. By 1910 Shaw wanted to resign from the Fabian executive, and wanted the other old guards to go too, but as Beatrice commented: 'All with the view to making room for the young men who are not there!' At this time, with Asquith's Liberal government in power and Lloyd George as Chancellor of the Exchequer, the government was embroiled in controversial legislation. The power of the House of Lords was to be dramatically reduced. Old Age Pensions were to be introduced. The Irish Home Rule question, in abeyance since the late 1880s, was about to be tackled again. Asquith's two most active ministers, Winston Churchill and David Lloyd George, did not have close links with the Fabian Society. Once again the Fabians were marginalised. In the hope of influencing the government, the Webbs formed the National Committee for the Prevention of Destitution, which, as Shaw pointed out, really made the Fabian Society redundant. In 1911 he resigned from the Fabian executive.

In the winter of 1910 Shaw crossed the Atlantic for the first time, but not to visit New York or Boston. He and Charlotte spent Christmas in Jamaica with their friend Sidney Olivier, once a Fabian colleague of Sidney Webb's in the Colonial Office, now the Governor General and a lord, living in the regal style still deemed requisite for the King-Emperor's representatives.

After the flop of the Frohman season, the 'highbrow' theatre returned to smaller houses, and Shaw's next play, 'Fanny's First Play', finished in March 1911, ran very successfully in the Little Theatre. An entertaining comedy, described by Shaw as a 'pot-boiler', it has a play within the play. This is written by the Fanny of the title, a modern young woman with a traditionalist, rich father. Fanny's play is as up-to-the-minute as anything by G. B. S., and its effect upon the Count, her father, is profound:

'Is this a play? Is this, in any sense of the word, Art? Is it agreeable? Can it conceivably do good to any human being? Is it delicate?'

– Shaw was able to enjoy mocking the more conservative reaction to his own work among the critics as well as the wider population, as the critics in the Epilogue to his play discuss the likely author of Fanny's work:

Bannal: . . . I believe it's Shaw.
Gunn: Rubbish!
Vaughan: Rot! You may put that idea out of your head, Bannal. Poor as this play is, there's the note of passion in it . . . Now I've repeatedly proved that Shaw is physiologically incapable of the note of passion.

There is a self-regarding note here, but the technique, managed with great skill, reveals why Shaw was seen as a master by such a playwright as Bertolt Brecht, who was to specialize in a drama that reminded the audience that it was watching a play, and deliberately cultivated a sense of alienation from the spectacle on the stage. As part of the mystification, the author's name was withheld at first, and

129

Shaw encouraged speculation that it was in fact by J. M. Barrie, who had recently had a huge success with 'Peter Pan'.

Barrie's play for children was partly what prompted Shaw's next work. He had thought 'Peter Pan' patronising to children, and claimed to have written 'Androcles and the Lion' 'to show what a play for children should be like'. Shaw's view of children was taken largely from his own self of some five decades previously, when as a boy he had read through *The Pilgrim's Progress, Gulliver's Travels, The Arabian Nights* and other works that twentieth-century children, with more immediately palatable fare to choose from, were happy to ignore. More directly, Shaw's new play targeted the very successful religious melodrama *The Sign of the Cross,* by Wilson Barrett. Subtitled 'A Fable Play', it takes the old story of Androcles, who took the thorn from the lion's foot, and attaches it to the time of the Roman persecution of the Christians. Androcles, a Christian, meets his lion again in the Roman arena, where it licks his hand instead of tearing him to shreds. The play is a mixture of burlesque comedy and serious thought, with many opportunities for Shavian comments on religion. But unlike a fable there is no moral to close with. Androcles, who enters the play with a lioness-like termagant of a wife, leaves it with an affectionate and docile lion as his companion. In 1916 Shaw wrote a massive preface to the published version, which is definitely not aimed at children and contains a long and reasoned account of the Gospels 'as they might be examined by an intelligent person who had recently heard of Christianity and was eager to discover its history and

doctrine and effect on human society' (St John Ervine).
'Androcles' was written in 1912, performed first in Berlin,
and not staged in London until late in 1913.

Throughout 1912 Shaw was physically out of sorts. The
headaches of his youth still plagued him. Certainly his
work-load was a drain on his physical strength. He was in
touch now with translators in Spain and France as well as
Germany, struggling to deal with interpretations of his
work in languages of which he had little or no grasp. An
American professor, Alexander Henderson, was writing his
biography, and Shaw was determined to keep an eye on
this project. There were all the usual calls on his time. But
there was something else as well. For the playwright who
had always had a weakness for a beautiful leading lady, a
new star had risen, in the person of Stella Tanner, better
known to the world as Mrs Patrick Campbell.

CHAPTER IX

THE PLAYWRIGHT AND THE ACTRESS

The relationship between Bernard Shaw and Mrs Patrick Campbell has become the stuff of myth and legend. Even those who know little of either personality often recount the famous supposed exchange when she proposed to him that they should produce a child together, since it was bound to be a prodigy, with his brains and her beauty. But what if it had her brains and his beauty, Shaw is supposed to have replied. (This was actually Shaw's response, by letter, to a later proposal from a European actress.) There are other tales of the two, equally mythical, but founded on a stratum of truth. For a time there was a deep mutual attraction, and on Shaw's part it went further than ever before.

Mrs Campbell was already a famous actress when Shaw began to take serious notice of her as a person, in 1912. As a star, she behaved in a way that was frequently more like a parody of the grand actress or prima donna. A crowd-puller capable of almost mesmeric performance, she was also a producer's nightmare. Her word had to be law. She had to be the focal point of every gathering, every event, which which she was involved. W. B. Yeats, who suffered from her temperament in the rehearsals for his play 'Deirdre', described her as having 'an ego like a raging tooth'. She had been on the stage since 1888, when she was 23, and had made her name in 'The Second Mrs Tanqueray'. She was a widow with two grown children; Mr Campbell had been killed in the Boer War. Shaw had long been aware of her as an actress of great presence and glamour, and had thought of her for many of his leading-lady parts. But, other than her reading the part of Cleopatra in the copyright performance of 'Caesar and Cleopatra', Mrs Campbell had never performed in a Shaw play. As far back as 1897, he had conceived a wonderful role for her, as an 'east end dona in an apron and three orange and red ostrich feathers'. It took a further fifteen years for the play to be written, but Shaw remained determined that Mrs Campbell, now forty-seven, should play his cockney flower-girl. The play was titled 'Pygmalion', after a legendary king of Cyprus who made a statue of a girl, and fell in love with it so deeply that Aphrodite brought it to life for him. Shaw read the play to Mrs Campbell; she liked it and agreed to take the part, and he fell in love with her – 'head over heels', he wrote to Granville Barker, 'violently and exquisitely'. He began writing her letters which both expressed and analysed his passion, and his boyish exuberance at the whole 'ridiculous and delightful' business extended to Charlotte, to whom he read his first (mostly about business) letters, explaining to Mrs Campbell that: 'My love affairs are her unfailing amusement: all their tenderness finally recoils on herself'. This was a wilful misrepresentation of the case. Charlotte had no doubt of the dangers that the siren-like actress had for the middle-aged playwright, and hustled him off on a motoring tour in the French Alps, with her sister.

Shaw continued to write to Stella, without showing any more letters to his wife; for much of the time he and Charlotte were apart, since following an accident, he and the driver took the car to its parent factory to be repaired. Unlike the Ellen Terry correspondence, where he had been in no hurry to meet her, the letters to Stella have an urgent quality. She had aroused in him feelings that took him right back to his boyhood, remembering how, in his teens 'I fell in love with a lady of your complexion'; and the supremely articulate Shaw was deprived of words to express what he felt: 'I dont know why: I cant write ... It is past letter writing with me'. He was serious, but she was less so. Shaw's reputation had gone before him; a friend had warned her: 'He walks into your heart with muddy galoshes, and then walks out, leaving his muddy galoshes behind him.' She was accustomed to the flushes of passion that are stimulated by the fervent collaboration and concentration of preparing a new play, and she knew that Shaw was solidly anchored to Charlotte – and she herself was engaged in a more serious relationship with a handsome socialite, George Cornwallis-West. It was all impossible, but Shaw pursued the impossible, with almost desperate sincerity, further than he ever had before.

He made assignations with Mrs Campbell at the house of his sister Lucy, who had never cared for Charlotte. Though Shaw financially maintained both his mother and his sister, relations between them and his wife were almost non-existent. Lucy was most unlikely to spill the beans. At this time too, in 1912, Shaw's emotional balance was assailed from another direction. His mother had suffered a stroke. Physically very strong, she survived two more attacks before her death in February 1913, at the age of eighty-two. In her latter years she had become a keen Spiritualist, doing automatic drawings while in a trance, and – in a surprising display of sentiment – trying to obtain 'spirit photographs' of her long-dead second child. Yet she informed Alexander Henderson, as he assiduously searched for documents on Shaw's life, that she had kept neither a photograph nor any letter of her son's. The mother's death precipitated a collapse by Lucy, who had been watching over the invalid for months (Shaw had also paid for the services of two nurses, and made regular visits himself). The only mourners at the cremation were Shaw and Granville Barker. The ever-inquiring Shaw went behind the scenes at the crematorium:

'... there was a plain chamber of cement and firebrick ... Then the violet coffin moved again and went in, feet first. And behold! The feet burst miraculously into streaming ribbons of garnet colored lovely flame, smokeless and eager, like pentecostal tongues, and as the whole coffin passed in it sprang into flame all over; and my mother became that beautiful fire.'

He waited to collect the ashes, then scattered them over a flower-bed. All this was related in a letter to Stella, the person to whom he felt he could open 'the grave of my childhood'. Granville Barker was astonished by Shaw's apparent lightheartedness, which St John Ervine explained as the only way Shaw knew of coping with profound emotion, and quotes other examples of flippancy in the face of serious or moving events. Undoubtedly the death of his mother released a flood of emotional pressure, all of it directed at the woman he loved. Often his letters to her refer to himself as a child, or with the needs of a child: 'to hear tones in a human voice that I have never heard before, to have it taken for granted that I am a child and want to be happy ...'

Mrs Campbell was herself ill at the time, and Shaw visited her regularly. Charlotte, who had assumed that he was attending committees or rehearsals, was furious when he told her, and took to her own bed for a time with a bronchial attack. Shaw tried, in his letters, to turn Charlotte's role into a sort of game, but Stella was not fooled. Realising that he would never actually abandon Charlotte, she became sarcastic, and a sense of rivalry developed between the 'middle-aged minx' and 'Mrs Mouse' as they referred to each other. Stella often tried to trick him into staying later with her than he meant to, so that Charlotte would be annoyed (one such scene is reproduced in 'The Apple Cart', when the King's mistress tries to make him late for a meeting with the Queen). Shaw, in his role as 'Mr Mouse' could not feel a heroic figure. Another name she had for him was 'Joey the Clown', though this was playful rather than contemptuous. He recognised the irony of his own predicament. This time, it was he who was love's victim. But unlike George Cornwallis-West, he was not prepared to divorce his wife. In June 1913 Stella told him she was intending to marry her other admirer. Shaw's response, in a letter, was defensive and jokey:

'... he is young and I am old, so let him wait until I am tired of you ... I will hurry through my dream as fast as I can; only let me have my dream out.'

Charlotte, now very much on the look-out for signs of divergence, found many. There were frequent stormy scenes. Once she overheard a telephone conversation between Shaw and Stella, and created such a storm that he felt: 'I must, it seems, murder myself or else murder her'. For a man who had successfully shut emotion from his life, it was a testing time. One day he found himself spontaneously crying: 'You may ask why I shouldnt cry; but it is not in my line: bad taste is what I am good at. Bad taste dries tears ...'

In August 1913, having seen Charlotte off on the boat-train to France – he was due to join her three weeks later – he went down to Kent, where he knew Stella had gone, and where she had forbidden him to follow. He tracked her to a hotel by Sandwich Bay. He was not the ironic, self-possessed G. B. S. After the long, emotionally gruelling courtship, he wanted to consummate their relationship. But Stella refused to admit him to her bed. She begged him to go back to London. 'Please don't make me despise you,' she wrote in a note to him. He was embarrassing, a frustrated would-be lover camped on her doorstep in a fashionable hotel. She feared the publicity and the reaction of Cornwallis-West to this unwelcome demonstration. In the end, because he would not go, she fled.

The effect on Shaw was shattering. He had exposed his vulnerability, revealed himself as a love-starved child, offered himself, only to be rejected. Not only rejected but made to

137

seem a fool – they had made a date to bathe together in the sea on the very morning she had decamped. He had cheerily turned up, and had to pretend he had got the date wrong – a fitting scene for Joey the Clown. In his bitterness he flung all kinds of accusations at her in a succession of letters – she had led him on, she was a 'one-part actress', a 'miserable wretch'. 'I want to hurt you because you hurt me,' he wrote.

That was the end of the dream. Back in London, business relations resumed, Mrs Patrick Campbell would duly play Eliza Doolittle in 'Pygmalion', and as Shaw had dully observed even in his first letter of agonised reproach, life went on: 'The sun shines: it is pleasant to swim: it is good to work ... ' But after this searing exposure to the irrational, involuntary, uncontrollable intensity of love, he relapsed into a heavily self-protective state, reflecting that 'the quantity of Love that an ordinary person can stand without serious damage is about ten minutes in fifty years.'

When Stella died, a lonely, forgotten and impoverished woman, in Paris in April 1940, he had long achieved detachment both from her and from the infatuated Shaw who had so ardently pursued her. He wrote to his friend Mrs Ada Tyrrell: 'Yes, she is dead, and everybody is greatly relieved ... she was not a great actress but she was a great enchantress ... She enchanted me among the rest; but I could not have lived with her for a week; and I knew it; so nothing came of it.'

In her later years, Stella had plagued him by wanting to publish his letters to her, not only for the money (he frequently sent her money) but because they would rekindle the world's memory of her greatest days. He was anxious to keep the letters private as long as his wife was alive; the lacerating scenes of jealous rage were not forgotten.

Beyond his own immediate circumstances, engrossing as they were, in 1913, Shaw with his ability to perceive general situations was more concerned than most by the drift towards a European war. He could clearly see the makings of conflict between Germany, an empire only since 1870 and determined to make its mark as a Great Power, and Britain, with its vast extent of imperial colonies and dominions. His proposal was a triple agreement, between the United Kingdom, France and Germany, so that '... if France attack Germany, we combine with Germany to crush France, and if Germany attack France, we combine with France to crush Germany.' It looked neat and sensible on paper like all Shavian schemes, but it was quite unrealistic in political and military terms. Shaw also proposed, 'as a Socialist' universal conscription with compulsory military service for all able-bodied persons. Many of his fellow-Socialists saw matters in quite a different way, with the coming war as a capitalist diversion from the true war of the classes which should unite the working people of Germany, Britain and all other countries; and they objected to the militarism on both sides of the North Sea (or German Ocean, as it was more often called).

During the period of self-examination within the Fabian Society provoked by H. G. Wells back in 1906, one of the gingering-up proposals had been that the Fabians should start up a magazine, in order to provide a more regular flow of opinion and argument than the occasional pamphlets. Nothing came of it at the time, but, with their invariable dedication, efficiency and energy, the Webbs got round to it eventually. The magazine, though it was intended to espouse Fabian values and Webbian causes, was not an official Fabian organ, but an independent publication, under the name of *The New Statesman*. Shaw made a handsome contribution of £1,000 to its start-up costs, and became a co-proprietor, despite considerable scepticism about the project, which he thought doomed to failure; and the first issue appeared in May 1913. Beatrice Webb had worked very hard to get him to participate, thus giving the new magazine, as she wrote to a potential subscriber, 'the wit of G. B. S. and the wisdom of the Webbs every week'.

This kind of sentiment was exactly what Shaw deplored, the sense that he was merely a big-name entertainer whose writings amused, whilst the real work of education and persuasion was done by others. He wanted to be both entertainer and persuader, and to be acknowledged as such. It was not long before he fell out with the new magazine, in the person of its editor, Clifford Sharp, hired by the Webbs for the correctness of his views on topics close to their hearts, like economic collectivism, but an uninspired journalist. Sharp sought a uniformity of tone for the magazine, and wanted all contributions to be anonymous save for those of Sidney Webb and Shaw, its two big guns (and in the case of Shaw, a uniquely recognisable vigour and style). Shaw, however, suspicious of the intention to treat him as an entertainer, wanted his articles to be anonymous in order to invest them with the authority of the movement as a whole. Even though they would be distinctively Shavian, they would cease to be individual. For exactly the same reason, Sharp resisted. This difference of opinion, combined with many other divergences of view between Sharp and Shaw, led to dissension.

Thanks to the industry of Shaw's faithful Austrian translator, Trebitsch, the first performance of 'Pygmalion' was in German, in the Hofburgtheater of Vienna, in October 1913, and was a great success. There was a further reason for the continental *première,* the commercial fear that German theatres might decline the play if it opened to a bad reception in London. The London staging, with Beerbohm Tree as Henry Higgins and Mrs Campbell (who had married George Cornwallis-West the week before) as Eliza, came in April 1914 and ran until July; in October it opened in New York, again with Mrs Campbell. It was to be one of Shaw's greatest international successes, long before it was transformed into a musical as 'My Fair Lady'. It was widely and breathlessly talked about, because Eliza at one point uses the phrase 'Not bloody likely.' Although this was not the first time 'bloody' had been used on the English stage as a swear-word, it was by far the most notorious: shock, demonstrations, fainting women, all had been predicted. When the moment came, St John Ervine relates, the audience gasped, then laughed and laughed again, although the Women's Purity League sent a deputation to protest to the Prime Minister. Although the play's ostensible theme is Shaw's pet subject of phonetics, its entertainment value happily obscures this. Shaw's character of Doolittle, the dustman prototype of the 'undeserving poor' who objects to being made middle-class, was a great hit, played by Edward Gurney.

In November 1914 the *New Statesman* published a supplementary pamphlet by Shaw, *Common Sense About the War*. It aroused a storm of controversy. At a time when most writers were resorting to patriotic sentiment, its tone of critical detachment infuriated many 'right-thinking' people. For some years he had been scornful of the 'my country right or wrong' attitude prevalent in Great Britain, and the general adulation of things naval and military. He had suggested in a *Daily News* article on January 1, 1914, that 'Those barbarians within our frontiers, who advocate war as a tonic, should not be let loose on foreigners but rather sent for annual war sports to Salisbury Plain, to blaze away at one another ...' Shaw was appalled by the anti–German hysteria and the blatantly false propaganda stories put out by the press and the government. Charlotte, a convinced pacifist, was completely opposed to war. Shaw believed the war to be as stupid and pointless as a fight between two quarrelsome dogs. (He also perceived some irony in the fact that the government, under pressure of war, had taken huge steps towards the kind of state control and nationalisation that he himself had preached in the wilderness for so long.)

If he had longed in the past to be taken seriously, instead of being regarded as a jester, he now found his ambition satisfied. His ironically phrased demands that people should question the purpose and aims of the war, that volunteer soldiers should have civil rights, his attack on the British Foreign Secretary, the elderly bird-watcher Sir Edward Grey, as a 'Junker', all brought a torrent of condemnation. Shaw believed that if Grey had categorically told Germany that Britain would fight in defence of Belgium or France, instead of fudging the issue, the war would not have happened. As a result of the pamphlet, he was regarded as a German sympathiser, if not an outright German agent, by many people. The playwright Henry Arthur Jones, a long-standing friend, became a bitter enemy, writing of him as 'you freakish homunculus, germinated outside of lawful procreation ...' Friends like Archer and Chesterton felt he had gone too far. Wells called him 'an elderly adolescent still at play.' It was only those who were wholly opposed to the war on principle, like Bertrand Russell, who gave him support. Shaw's reaction to this outrage was to present a front both of magnanimity and insouciance. He did not join the likes of Henry Arthur Jones in the gutter. To Wells he wrote: 'The longer I live the more I see that I am never wrong about anything.' He brought all his own india-rubber bounce and irrepressibility to bear against the vilification. No one could say any more that Shaw was just a cynical writer who postured to get laughs. Under pressure from angry patriots, he withdrew from two committees in the Society of Authors, a body in which he had been a key figure (he once wrote that, when fighting in defence of his fellow-writers, he had found a back-plate to be much more necessary than a breast-plate); and resigned from the Dramatists' Club, where a majority of members refused to accept him at their regular lunches.

Someone who might have supported him was Harley Granville Barker, the man to whom Shaw felt closest both as a person and a theatre colleague. But Barker was having problems of his own. In the USA he had fallen in love with a wealthy married woman, Helen Huntington. This was not only to wreck his marriage to Lillah McCarthy, but to end his stage career – Helen did not care for the theatre and even less for theatre folk. Shaw, and Charlotte even more so, disapproved of his treatment of Lillah. The friendship proved unequal to the strains, and to Shaw's long-lasting regret, they ceased to stay in touch with each other.

It was Shaw's awareness of being an Irishman rather than an Englishman, or a Briton, that helped him towards the 'plague on both your houses' view of the First World War that so enraged the English. With a mind that viewed events in terms of Great Powers and the advances and retreats of huge, intangible forces like Capitalism and Socialism; that could embrace the fall of empires, he passed little comment on what seemed a short-lived revolutionary attempt, by some not very well-known people, in his own native city at Easter 1916. The Easter Rising, which prompted a profound and prophetic response from W. B. Yeats (who was much more closely involved both with Dublin and with some of the personalities concerned) was not of special importance to Shaw. Though he did protest that the sixteen men shot in Dublin should have been treated as prisoners of war, an outburst of flippancy also came, in which he announced: 'How I wish I had been in command of the British artillery on that fatal field! How I should have improved my native city!' He refused to contribute to the cost of defending Sir Roger Casement, who was put on trial in London. He thought Casement should conduct his own defence, as Robert Emmet had done a century before, and provided Casement's main supporter, Alice Green, with a speech for Casement to make. The remarks, intended for the prisoner to utter, do not necessarily reflect Shaw's own attitude, but their common sense suggests his approval:

144

'Almost all the disasters and difficulties that have made the relations of Ireland with England so mischievous to both countries have arisen from the failure of England to understand that Ireland is not a province of England, but a nation, and to negotiate with her on that assumption. If you persist in treating me as an Englishman, you bind yourself thereby to hang me as a traitor before the eyes of the world. Now as a simple matter of fact, I am neither an Englishman nor a traitor: I am an Irishman, captured in a fair attempt to achieve the independence of my country ...'

The tone is low-key; Shaw's emotion was not engaged. Even so, the effect on an English judge and jury of such remarks, in mid-1916, would not have been a positive one, though loyally Charlotte Shaw wrote (ten years later) to T. E. Lawrence to relate that Casement had used Shaw's draft in his speech after sentence had been passed, and 'several of the jury said afterwards that if they had heard all that before retiring the verdict would have been different'. As it was, Casement's knighthood was rescinded, and he was hanged.

It was late in 1916 before some of the more thoughtful commentators began to acknowledge that there was indeed common sense in Shaw's comments on the war. By then military conscription had been introduced, prompting a somewhat confused response from Shaw, considering his views on service to the state: he spent much time helping to defend and justify the position of those who objected to being pressed into the army, on grounds of conscience. In January 1917 he received a surprising official invitation to visit the Western Front and see the war at first hand. Prepared to be sceptical and see only 'the conventional round' of a public-relations tour, he found himself asked what he wanted to see; and also came to realise that the impact of total war on a landscape and an army could not be concealed. His reaction was a strange blend of philosophical thought and almost flippant-seeming comment. He admired the collective spirit in which the army behaved: 'trying to get things done in the best possible way for the benefit of your comrades-in-arms, of your country, of the whole of which you are a part ...' and comparing that spirit unfavourably to the competitive ethos of commerce. But the Shaw who could write, after the war, of his own horror at the destructiveness of such battles as Festubert; of public indifference to the slaughter of common soldiers and the same public's exaggerated horror at the deaths of the 'saloon passengers on the *Lusitania*', also wrote that 'the Somme battlefield was very much safer than the Thames Embankment with its race of motors and trams'. His experiences included a visit to Ypres under bombardment, lunch with the Commander-in-Chief, and an amateur performance of two of his own most recent one-act plays, 'O'Flaherty VC', and 'The Inca of Perusalem', put on by men commanded by his friend Robert Loraine, now a major in the Royal Flying Corps. He saw one dead body. As 'Joyriding at the Front', his account was an effort at black humour which fails dismally; he had found his tour, as he wrote to Lady Gregory, to be a demoralising experience.

*T*HE PESSIMISTIC OPTIMIST

During the war years Shaw wrote only one major play, whose working title was 'The House in the Clouds' but which became 'Heartbreak House'.

Lady Gregory, visiting the Shaws in November 1916, noted in her diary that he had read her the first act, 'very amusing', but that he had said he did not know how to finish it. The performance he had seen in France of 'O'Flaherty VC' was the only wartime production of a play which had been begun, in 1915, to encourage Irishmen to join up in the British army. Unfortunately for this purpose, when complete, it turned out to be much more of a criticism of Ireland, Irish people, and war in general, than a recruiting play. On the advice of the authorities, it was not produced in Dublin. The play is expressive of Shaw's ambivalence about Ireland, and O'Flaherty himself has more than a whiff of Synge's 'playboy', Christy Mahon, about him; but it is a lightweight piece. However, the Abbey put on a whole series of his plays, with great success, in late 1916 and early 1917.

'Heartbreak House', labelled as a 'political play' by Shaw, is 'cultured, leisured Europe before the war' according to its preface, written in 1919, and Shaw explicitly relates it to the dramatic landscape of Chekhov's 'The Cherry Orchard' and his other plays. Although he does not employ the analogy, his characters are like the passengers on the *Titanic,* rich, clever, cultured, but basically disengaged from reality and unaware of impending catastrophe. This preface has a sad-angry tone far removed from conventional Shavian verbal fireworks. The play had not been performed; despite the huge increase in theatre-going during the war, the theatre of ideas had not benefited (and Shaw's plays in particular were boycotted by managements earlier in the war). The war was over, but Shaw had found that, as the German philosopher Hegel had said long before, all we learn from history is that we learn nothing from history. Shaw did not write plays about the war, he says, because:

'When men are heroically dying for their country, it is not the time to shew their lovers and wives and fathers and mothers how they are being sacrificed to the blunders of boobies, the cupidity of capitalists, the ambition of conquerors, the elec-tioneering of demagogues, the Pharisaism of patriots, the lusts and lies and rancors and bloodthirsts that love war ...'

The play ends to the sound of heavy explosions and the breaking of windows. To some, the noise is exhilarating:

Mrs Hushabye: Did you hear the explosions? And the sound in the sky: it's splendid: it's like an orchestra: it's like Beethoven.
Ellie: By thunder, Hesione: it is Beethoven.

– But it is not – it is the crack of doom above Heartbreak House and its illusions.

In the immediate post-war years, Shaw was in a gloomy mood much of the time. Disgusted by the attitude of the 'winners' in the post-war settlement, chastened perhaps more than he would reveal by the Stella affair and by the events of the war itself, he was depressed by the failure of 'Heartbreak House' when it was brought to the London stage in 1921; it had previously opened very successfully in New York. Of all his plays it was the one he himself had most respect for (there was a memorable row in Oxford in 1923 when he mounted the stage in fury to solemnly and publicly curse an Oxford Players' production that managed to turn his 'semi-tragedy' into what he termed a bedroom farce). The fall of Tsarist Russia and the establishment of the Soviet State were welcomed by him as an internationally minded Socialist, but his attention was more on Western Europe and the mess that was being made of it.

In March 1920 his last remaining close relative, his sister Lucy, died. Shaw was with her when she died, recording:

'When I had sat with her a little while, she said, "I am dying." I took her hand to encourage her and said, rather conventionally, "Oh, no; you will be all right presently." We were silent then; and there was no sound except from somebody playing the piano in the nearest house (it was a fine evening and all the windows were open) until there was a very faint flutter in her throat. She was still holding my hand. Then her thumb straightened. She was dead.'

149

In this strange togetherness ended the family nexus that he had lived in ever since 'Sonny's' first awareness of life at home in Dublin. Lucy's normal attitude to him had been one of hostility and jealousy; she had regarded herself as the artist and him as a cashier who did not know his place; later she had claimed credit for some of his ideas while managing to pour cold water on his success. She was bitter about life in her latter years. But, as with his mother, the cold record does not tell the whole story. Shaw often thought about Lucy – writing long after her death, he mentioned about Mrs Campbell that 'she was very kind to Lucy' – he supported her in her divorce and afterwards. At some level, there was a genuine bond, a sense of recognition; not in affection but in the bone and gristle of kinship and shared experience from the shaping years: they were both the children of George Carr Shaw and Lucinda Gurly. Both could have entertained the same thought – his fate might have been hers, the tragedy of talent without character; and hers might have been his, the heroi-comic winning of a success that he himself eternally questioned.

'She will tell you lies about my childhood,' Shaw had said to Stella, when the latter proposed to go and visit the invalid Lucy. His childhood was now his own exclusive property, except that more people wanted to write biographies of him. At this time his interest in Ireland developed a hitherto unknown intensity. As Joyce recorded, and Yeats and Beckett also demonstrated, Irish writers' relations with their country were often strained, and self-chosen exile was their natural condition to stay free of 'the old sow that eats her farrow'. Encouraged by Charlotte, whose interest in Ireland was always greater than his own and who had a leaning towards nationalist rather than the unionist, or more exactly 'federated home rule' beliefs of her husband, stimulated by the success of his 1916–17 season at the Abbey Theatre, and with his interest sharpened by the post–1918 political developments, Shaw wrote to Lady Gregory:'I am an Irishman and I have not forgotten'. He took up Irish causes, like the struggle to have Hugh Lane's last wish honoured by transferring the bequest of his magnificent picture collection to Dublin, and advised the Irish on their political difficulties. He had greatly regretted that Lloyd George had refused to nominate him to the Convention on Irish Home Rule set up in 1917, because he believed that his solution, a federation of 'the four home kingdoms' was a unique one. Instead he wrote newspaper articles, published later as *How To Settle The Irish Question*. Events moved on without him. He and Charlotte dined with Michael Collins in a country house, Kilteragh, two days before he was ambushed and shot in August 1922. The owner of Kilteragh was Sir Horace Plunkett, who had tried to be the broker of Ireland's future in the Convention and who was now looking with helpless distress on the fact that a war of independence was now turning into a civil war. The Shaws frequently visited Ireland in those years, claiming, with echoes of his remarks on the Somme, that it was safer than most other places. Shaw was recruited by Plunkett to play a part in promoting his moderate Dominion League, but all chances of moderation were being destroyed by the semi–official activities of the Black–and–Tans. Shaw, of Irish Protestant stock, was dismayed by Lloyd George's proposal to retain six counties of Ulster within the United Kingdom;

his vision of Ireland had always been that of a single nation. With Yeats, he became a reluctant supporter of the agreement reached by Griffiths and Collins with Lloyd George in 1921, with Dominion status, but excluding six of the counties of Ulster. In the summer of 1922, Shaw announced that the Irish situation was impossible. He wrote in the *Daily Express:* 'Mr de Valera does not know how to play his hand; and … I had better play the hand for him.' Mr de Valera did not however trouble to ask for Mr Shaw's advice. After 1923, Shaw did not return to Ireland, though he did not forget he was an Irishman, and he was not finished with his native country yet.

In 1920 he completed the work which he regarded as his most considered achievement, the hugely long 'Back to Methuselah', made up of five parts of varying length. In its first production, in New York (February 1922) it took a week to perform the full cycle, and it was estimated to lose its producers $20,000. With a comfortable flow of royalties coming in, Shaw could afford the time and the indulgence of writing a work that was so grandly uncommercial. The play begins with Adam, Eve and the Serpent in the Garden of Eden, and ends on a summer afternoon in 31920AD. The play was written to express a number of its writer's crucial beliefs. Among these were his concept of the evolutionary Life-Force, now given a sufficient span to demonstrate itself; the imperfection of creation and its striving towards the state which would produce a god who is all-powerful and all-knowing; his belief in the ability of the human will to achieve its desired ends; his sense that life is not long enough for even the longest-lived person to properly apply learned experience. Above all, it is an attack on what he refers to in the play as 'discouragement', in the preface as 'despair', and which had a close resemblance to the medieval sin of *accidie* – embracing sloth, cynicism, world-weariness, casual immorality – which he saw evidence of all around him. Though he makes no reference to Teilhard de Chardin, he shared a similar view to that of the French religious scientist, that evolution is not the 'Darwinian' process of survival of the fittest, but a mental progress; one of Shaw's characters in Part 5, the She-Ancient, even explains: 'The day will come when there will be no people; only thought,' a state exactly analogous to Teilhard's concept of a single mass-consciousness. With Shaw the process can easily go beyond man: 'Man may easily be beaten: Evolution will not be beaten.' The thought behind the Methuselah cycle owes most, however, to Samuel Butler (1835–1902), author of *Erewhon* and *The Way of All Flesh,* whose satirical style and refusal to accept Darwin's banishing of mind from the universe had a strong effect on Shaw.

From the premise that certain persons in the Old Testament lived for centuries, with Methuselah holding the record at 969, Shaw elaborates his drama in which some of the characters are hundreds of years old, and people of sixty are considered to be still in the stage of childhood. By the year 3000, humanity has separated into the long-livers and short-livers; although the two groups seem to speak the same language, in fact they scarcely understand one another. The long-lived inhabit a remote set of islands, once known as the British Isles, where the short-livers come to consult their superior wisdom; and they themselves debate the alternatives of remaining apart, or of colonising the world and in the process destroying the short-livers. The final part, 'as far as thought can reach' depicts the ultimate society of the long-livers. Sex, copulation, love, as known to their remote ancestors, play no part in their lives. Hatched from eggs at the age of sixteen, they have a period of childhood which equates to most of the actual human life-span, before becoming 'Ancients' still with centuries of life ahead of them. On the face of it these ancients, hairless, sexless, unappealing to look at, don't have much to occupy or fulfil their existences, but one of them explains to a questioning 'child': 'Infant: one moment of the ecstasy of life as we live it would strike you dead.'

For the orthodox Christian, of course, such spiritual intensity awaits in Heaven, but Heaven was no part of Shaw's scheme of things.

'Back To Methuselah', with its tremendous visionary sweep, full of incidental satire and humour, was a great success in book form, though its carefree references in Part 3 to 'niggers' and 'Chinks' demonstrate how far social awareness has moved in seventy years. Shaw had been amazed by the fact that the American Theatre Guild had put the play on; and was even more surprised when Barry Jackson, patron of the Birmingham Repertory Theatre, staged it there in late 1923, in a production greatly enjoyed by the playwright. When he had completed 'Methuselah', by then sixty-five years old himself, he said to St-John Ervine that he was finished. But, Ervine reminds us, he went on to write 'Saint Joan'.

In fact, nearly thirty years later, he would still be writing plays.

Joan of Arc, the inspired peasant girl who had led the French army to victory, raised the siege of Orleans, crowned the king, been handed over to the English and burned by them as a heretic, had been the subject of a number of recent plays and musical dramas. Even the great American humorist Mark Twain had had a go at her. Several people suggested the theme to Shaw as a good one for him, including the person to whose quietly murmured advice he was always most receptive, his wife. Reading the translated transcripts of Joan's trial, he became convinced, and wrote it rapidly in the course of 1923. During that year he read the play to the actress Sybil Thorndike and her husband Lewis Casson, who he hoped would play its leading roles. She was entranced from the first:

'Shaw read divinely. Like an actor, but much bigger size than most actors ... one could see why he had wanted so passionately to write it. He made it clear that Joan did for France then what we hope somebody may yet do for the world.'

'Saint Joan' was first performed in New York, in December 1923, and became a great popular success, though not without some anxious moments for its backers when some of the first-night audience left early and the critical verdicts were very mixed. It remains Shaw's most popular and widely read and performed play, and it was in large part as the author of 'Saint Joan' that he was awarded the Nobel Prize for Literature in 1926.

Shaw was reluctant to accept the Nobel Prize. Unlike W. B. Yeats, who had been the laureate in 1923, and who found the money welcome, he did not need the money, and he had a wholesome reluctance to accept any public honours of a ceremonial kind. In a graceful return compliment to Sweden, he applied the £7,000 prize money to establishing a fund for making Swedish literature available in English. The award, in his seventieth year, confirmed his status as something more than a playwright and polemicist of genius. He became a Grand Old Man, an institution, part of the fabric of people's daily lives, regarded with some affection even by many who abhorred most of his ideas, striking out predictably in his own well-known causes like an ancient and well-kept grandfather clock ticking away in the nation's front hall. He was growing detached from the world in inevitable ways. In 1924 William Archer died, and he lost one of his closest friends and the man who had been his literary conscience. His correspondence with his boyhood friend Matthew MacNulty had petered out, though MacNulty was among the numerous friends and associates to write a Shavian memoir. Charlotte and his secretary provided an effective screen against most, if not quite all, of the people who wanted to meet him. But he did make new friends, or new people made friends with him, including the dynamic Lady Astor, the first woman to sit in the Westminster Parliament as an MP, and a political-social hostess on the grand scale in the Astor mansion of Cliveden, just west of London. It was important that Charlotte also liked Nancy Astor. Charlotte Shaw was even more impressed by T. E. Lawrence, who treated Shaw himself as a sage and guru, sending him the manuscript of *Seven Pillars of Wisdom* and anxiously awaiting a long-deferred but favourable judgment. Charlotte's correspondence with 'Lawrence of Arabia' was more intense and personal than her husband's. Having already taken over one man of genius, it is tempting to speculate that a younger Charlotte might have done the same for Lawrence, but he was an utterly different person to Shaw. Shaw and Charlotte bought him a motorbike, though an earlier model than the one on which he was to suffer his fatal accident in 1935. A friendship which Charlotte found much less to her taste was that between Shaw and Molly Tompkins, a beautiful young American with a wealthy and, for a long time, complaisant husband, who simply took the eminent dramatist by storm in 1921, having crossed the Atlantic, she said, to find him. Something about Shaw – his outspokenness perhaps; his reputation for replying to all communications; not least his constant public pronouncements on a host of issues both central and peripheral to the interests of other people – made him a target for a host of correspondents who wanted advice, encouragement, money. There was something patriarchal about Shaw, though he was the father only of a host of ideas, that encouraged people into his shadow, as if touching his mantle would give them knowledge, wisdom, or peace. Molly, beset by vague ambitions to be an actress, or a scupltress, was more pushy than most, and for twenty years was to remain a restive, irritating but also tolerated and sporadically encouraged presence in his life. The shades of Janet Achurch, Florence Farr, even Jenny Patterson, rose again; and Molly had a distinct physical resemblance to Stella Campbell in her prime. For her part, Molly's adulation became a genuine affection for Shaw; and at times a physical passion which the elderly playwright warded off with some embarrassment and difficulty.

Beatrice Webb observed the 'social' friendships of the Shaws with a wry interest, seeing them as further instances of Shaw's detachment from serious Socialist politics. But if no longer actively involved in politics, Shaw, who in the 1940s still considered himself a 'vociferous Marxist Communist', had not lost his interest in world affairs. At the unlikely behest of his sister-in-law, now Lady Cholmondely, who wanted a few notes on what Socialism was about for her ladies' study circle, he wrote the more than 200,000-word long *The Intelligent Women's Guide to Socialism and Capitalism*. The hint of patronage in the title was unintended. The publication, in 1927, proved timely, since in the following year, women in the United Kingdom were at last given the vote on the same terms as men, and the 'flapper vote' was presumed to be heavily influenced by Shaw's guide to Socialism.

The *Guide* argued in favour of egalitarianism and democracy, but within a strongly centralised, government-led society. Shaw's views on this had altered little with the passing of the years, but they had an old-fashioned look to some left-wing thinkers who were concerned by Lenin's methods of government in Russia and by the growth of the Fascist movement in Italy. Shaw admired Mussolini, who by mid-1924 had established himself as the dictator of Italy. Again with the grand and long-term view, he saw the Italian dictator, and, later, Hitler, as agents of a larger process towards reform; and he registered his own feelings in writing, as people often do when defending the indefensible, on behalf of anonymous others: those others being 'so tired of indiscipline and muddle and Parliamentary deadlock, that they feel the need of strenuous tyranny'. This was political pragmatism from which the sense of necessary morality had become separated.

While Shaw was engaged in his political guide, the long-established London base of Adelphi Terrace had to be changed. St John Ervine, by now a friend, found them a flat next to his own in a stately block, Whitehall Court, in Westminster. Life alternated between here and Shaw's Corner, with forays to country houses; and, after 1923, a resumption of foreign travels (it was in Madeira that he heard of Archer's death). Another new device to which Shaw took with enthusiasm was the radio. Ever the propagandist and teacher, he realised that here was a way in which his speeches, both those delivered by himself and those delivered by his characters, could be heard, not by hundreds, but by millions. He gave many radio talks, and, as with his platform speeches, he asked for no fee. The BBC, however, under its severely correct director-general, Sir John Reith, kept him within bounds, and refused to broadcast his seventieth-birthday talk, 'Socialism at Seventy' because it was too politically controversial, annoying Shaw but giving him also some gratification in feeling that he was not tamed by either age or fame.

The succession of political and financial crises between 1929 and 1931 accentuated Shaw's sense of the muddle and lack of direction of the party-political process. He admired the personality of Sir Oswald Mosley, who resigned from the Labour Party in 1931 to form the New Party, which soon became the British Union of Fascists. While Yeats in Ireland flirted with General O'Duffy and the Blueshirts, Shaw was tantalised in England by the thought of what a strong man could achieve (Mosley himself was deeply influenced by Shaw's concept of the Superman and certainly saw himself, to some degree, as a Shavian hero). In 1932, in a speech to celebrate the anniversary of Guy Fawkes's attempt to blow up the Houses of Parliament, Shaw talked about what would happen 'the moment things begin seriously to break up ... I do not say that Sir Oswald Mosley is going to become Dictator of this country, though more improbable things have happened ...' Shaw might have better appreciated the huge inertia, or stability, of British society, which meant that, despite the dire economic and messily unsatisfactory political situation, things did not in fact break up. He was not attracted to the Fascists' political creed or to their style of politics, but his criticisms were relatively muted; and most leftwing thinkers regarded him as a lost ally, or a spent force, from then on.

Paradoxically, as his influence in political circles waned, his popular esteem and readership continued to swell. Far from the uncertainties and high rents of London's West End, the theatrical impresario and producer Sir Barry Jackson established the Malvern Festival at Great Malvern, a holiday town more than a hundred miles west of London. Jackson's aim was to make Shaw's work the centrepiece of the annual festival, and for the inaugural season of August 1929 Shaw wrote his first new play in five years, a political drama, 'The Apple Cart'. In this play, subtitled 'A Political Extravaganza', set in a fictitious Britain, King Magnus, the hero, is a man of intelligence, initiative and action – just the sort of person to be at the helm of a nation-state. He is contrasted with a government of mostly incompetent and inept politicians, among whom the only effective people are the women. Locked in dispute with his government, and accused of abusing his position as a democratic monarch, Magnus checkmates his opponents by offering to abdicate and stand against them in a general election: they know he will beat them at their own game.

In 1931 Shaw went to Russia with Lord and Lady Astor and one or two others, a little group of the great and good, to see Stalin's state at first hand. When they were granted a long meeting with the Soviet dictator, Lady Astor was bold enough to ask him why he had kept on shooting Russians; his answer was one Shaw might have written for him – 'When peace comes we shall stop it'. These deaths were necessary so that the Communist State could be established. Ever since Lenin had taken control, Shaw had been a defender of and apologist for the Communist state, partly in reaction to the hyperbolic anti-Bolshevik utterances of writers like Winston Churchill, who had described Lenin in terms of a plague bacillus. But Shaw was perfectly well aware that ten years would not transform a huge empire into even a remote resemblance to the Marxist dream-state. Taken on a carefully controlled tour, the eminent visitors saw Moscow and Leningrad (as it then was), schools, theatres, power stations, factories. They met the Communist writer Maxim Gorki, already at odds with the effects of the revolution he had helped to make; and saw a production of Bertolt Brecht's play 'The Threepenny Opera': 'amazing and perverse' was Shaw's comment on the adaptation of Gay's 'The Beggars' Opera' by a playwright who owed much of

161

his own technique to the succession of German productions of Shaw's own plays. Impressed by his visit, Shaw said to a public meeting just before he left:

'It is a real comfort to me, an old man, to be able to step into my grave with the knowledge that the civilization of the world will be saved . . .'

– and he returned invigorated and full of enthusiasm, not at all the exhausted wreck anticipated by the anxiously waiting Charlotte.

CHAPTER XI

THE WORLD TRAVELLER

Shaw liked to believe that Communism in Russia was a form of religion, replicating the structure of the Catholic Church without its crippling belief in private property (including its own). This is the kernel of the preface to his next play, 'Too True To Be Good', written after the Russian jaunt and premiered at Malvern in 1932. The first play to feature a live Microbe as one of the characters, its ebullience and humour reflect the sense of uplift Shaw had got from Russia. Its almost surreal episodes confused many critics but some Shaw admirers, like Lawrence Langner, of the New York Theatre Guild, thought it 'probably the finest acting thing that G. B. S. has ever made'. It was not however a West End success when it transferred to London, renewing Shaw's view that 'the case for a National Theatre grows stronger as the commercial theatres flourish more and more and raise the standard of expenditure . . .' Serious theatre was finding it hard to compete with high-budget musical shows and other stage spectaculars.

The Shaws' travels were now extending well beyond Europe. In December 1931 they sailed to South Africa. With all the colonial enthusiasm for meeting a celebrity, he was received with immense interest and enthusiasm by the white English-speaking population. But Shaw had not come to be adulated as a phenomenon. After four weeks, broadcasting across the country, he said of his time there: 'I felt that I was in a Slave State, and that, too, the very worst sort of Slave State', and he forecast the moral decline of South African whites until 'civilization breaks down through idleness and loafing based on slavery ...'

The South African stay was lengthened when Shaw's always-hazardous driving brought about a road accident in a hired car which caused serious injuries to Charlotte. Waiting for her to recuperate, he began work on one of his more curious works, *The Adventures of the Black Girl in Her Search for God*. Modelled in part on Voltaire's *Candide,* drawing on his South African observation, and fulfilling a long-held urge to express his view that Christianity, as propounded by St Paul, had completely misrepresented the life of Christ by its emphasis on his death instead of on his life and teaching, this was another intelligent person's guide from Shaw-the-guru. The Black Girl, her innocence and ignorance both exemplified by her nakedness, told by a missionary that to find God she must seek him, proceeds to do just that, in a magic jungle where all forms of religion conveniently lurk in order to be annihilated in the face of innocent questioning, until she meets a red-haired Irishman, digging in a very Voltairean garden. They fall in love, and the hunt for God is ended in human happiness and the production of coffee-coloured children in fulfilment of the aims of the Life-Force. The ending was also intended to show what Shaw believed to be the solution to the racial problem, inter-marriage: 'The future is to the mongrel ... I, Bernard Shaw, have said it.' The oddest response to the *Black Girl* was the proposal from a member that Shaw, as its author, should be expelled from the County Wexford Bee-Keepers' Association (the proposal was rejected). The book also cost Shaw an unusual friendship, that with the Abbess of Stanbrook Abbey in Worcestershire. He had been introduced to her by his friend Sir Sydney Cockerell, and came regularly to see her in her enclosed Benedictine order. She recognised the spirituality of 'Brother Bernard', but her conservatism could not accept his new book, and she was angered by his note on the presentation copy that it had come 'in response to the prayers of the nuns at Stanbrook Abbey.' She would have nothing more to do with him. But, more than a year later, by a misunderstanding, he believed she had died, and wrote a heart-felt letter of condolence to the Abbey. To his surprise, she answered in person, and their friendship resumed.

In 1932 the Shaws were on board ship again, this time on a four month world cruise which took them to India, China, Japan, and, for the first time in Shaw's case, to the United States. Shaw, who had met Mahatma Gandhi in London, was in favour of Indian independence on much the same lines as he had once favoured for Ireland. Gandhi was in jail at the time of Shaw's visit (he never went beyond Bombay). Two of his old loves had gone to the East; Florence Farr had died in Ceylon, and Annie Besant was in India, the leader of the Theosophists; she was to die that same year.

During that year he somewhat reluctantly accepted the presidency of the newly established Irish Academy of Letters, another manifestation of W. B. Yeats's concern to develop and foster a genuine Irish literary culture. 'I am really a London man', protested Shaw, who remained president until 1935, when Yeats took over. But the Irish Academy did not engage his interest as the Society of Authors did – the presidency was a gesture, though one which greatly pleased Charlotte, as did another gesture when, after the Irish Republic was declared in 1938, he registered himself as one of its citizens.

Once upon a time, the young Shaw had thought of emigrating to the United States. Since his fame, despite warm and repeated invitations, he had never visited the country, though he had set two plays there and incorporated several American characteres in the casts of others. There was a deep ambivalence in the Communist guru's view of the land where Capitalism was king; here too in its way was 'a colossal social experiment'. His brief stay began in the palace of San Simeon, the vast house of the press tycoon William Randolph Hearst. It was followed by a flying visit to Hollywood, already well-established as the movie capital and a place which Shaw detested for its triteness, commercialism and hypocritical values. The Hollywood producers saw in Shaw a valuable property, but he had no intention of allowing himself to be caught. They sailed down the West Coast, through the Panama Canal, and up to New York, where he was to give a single lecture, at the Metropolitan Opera House. Speaking to 3,500 people, his subject 'The Political Madhouse in America and Nearer Home', Shaw attacked two of the foundations of the American Dream: Hollywood, 'the most immoral place on earth', and New York City itself, where he pinned on the Wall Street financier and the cheap street crook the same label of 'racketeers'. His audience would have expected no less, but the reception was never-theless a somewhat muted one.

Eschewing the pleasures of shipboard life, Shaw wrote a short play during the cruise, 'The Village Wooing', and fol-lowed it up quickly when home again, with 'On The Rocks', a 'Political Comedy' in which the ineffectual Prime Minister of the first Act, Sir Arthur Chavender, undergoes the ministrations of a mysterious woman doctor to become, in the second Act, a hero for a time – the man with the an-swers. But he has come to recognise his true self and his in-capacity to change things. As he tells his distraught wife:

'Why dont I lead the revolt against it all? Because Im not the man for the job, darling; and nobody knows that better than you. And I shall hate the man who will carry it through for his cruelty and the desolation he will bring on us and our like.'

That dialectic, between the need for action and the drastic results of the action itself, obsessed the thought of Shaw in his last years. There was a further element to stir his feelings, too. As he looked back on his own lengthy career, he could share the thought expressed by Sir Arthur Chavender:

'I am enjoying the enormous freedom of having found myself out and got myself off my mind. Do you think I didnt know, in the days of my great speeches and my roaring popularity, that I was only whitewashing the slums?'

167

Shaw too had made great speeches; he had seen the failure of Fabianism, the failure of capitalism, the failure of the Labour Party, the failure of the working people of England to rise against exploitation and misery. He had felt the failure of G. B. S., the role he had created for himself, to be truly effective. Gandhi, a man who inspired, led and altered the lives of tens of millions, called him the Arch-jester, thinking to pay a compliment, but recognising the talent to amuse rather than the earnestness to bring about change. Shaw wanted to be a fierce old man who told terrible truths; and found instead that he was petted and feted. 'It's G. B. S.,' they might say. 'There's no harm in him.'

In his prefaces to his last plays he brooded on terrible actions. That of 'On the Rocks' (1933) contemplates Extermination: 'Extermination must be put on a scientific basis if it is ever to be carried out humanely and apologetically as well as thoroughly.'

Shaw, who was born less than a hundred years after Voltaire died, could not summon even the scant philosophical consolation of the eighteenth century. 'Cultivate your garden' made no sense when the Russian land-owning peasants were being wiped out. Pronouncing his optimism about the Life-Force steadily improving on itself, he had lived into a time when the twentieth century was proving that human cruelty on an individual and mass scale could match or exceed anything that had gone before.

But writing was his game – 'a Platonic exercise' he called it in a letter to Mrs St John Ervine, and he continued to write. During the long journey to New Zealand and back, in 1934, he wrote three plays, 'The Simpleton of the Unexpected

Isles', 'The Millionairess' and 'The Six of Calais'. Despite a recent law enabling the government to ban Communist sympathisers from entering the country, New Zealand gave him celebrity treatment. He found it an intriguing society, 'like a growing child', and 'the best country I've been in.' He did not spare their prejudices, but liked the way they listened to him; and enjoyed their un-stuffy approach to life both in-doors and in the open air.

The three plays written on board ship had a mixed recep-tion and were indeed a varied trio. 'The Simpleton' was set in the cleverly conceived Unexpected Isles, recently risen from the depths of the Pacific, and used as the setting for a fantastic comedy of ideas set around some of Shaw's favour-ite social themes: parents and children, marriage, love, reli-gion and eugenics all contribute to its bizarre story, which is interrupted half-way through by a Judgement Day very dif-ferent from that in the Book of Resurrection, treating it not as the end of the world, but the end of the world's child-hood. 'The Six of Calais' is a one-act historical joke-play, turning the historical story of the six martyr-burghers of Calais into a happy-ending romp. In 'The Millionairess', the playwright is back on ground familiar to his admirers – St John Ervine calls it 'the later life of Blanche Sartorius', the heroine of 'Widowers' Houses'; and this story of the richest woman in the world, whose money-making tests for poten-tial husbands have brought her only discontent and despair, and who at last finds happiness with a Muslim doctor who cares nothing for money, was a great success. Its form was traditional, it provided a splendid vehicle for a leading ac-tress, and its underlying concept, though perfectly Shavian,

169

had none of the complex and allegorical presentation that baffled the audiences of 'The Simpleton'.

He was now nearing the age of eighty, and still working at a pace and with a regularity that few men of his age could equal. On 24th November, 1934, he suffered a mild heart attack. Writing after this to one of his oldest friends, the Fabian Henry Salt, he said it was the greatest pity that he had revived. If that had been death, it would have been got over with speed and suddenness. But he found himself still alive, with death, in whatever form it might choose to take, still to anticipate. Though he described himself and Charlotte as 'both slightly dotty with age', his mind remained sharp. Unlike the great majority of old people, he found that his brain remained in good fettle, but his body let him down. In 1936, he and Charlotte undertook what was to be their last ocean cruise, into the Pacific Ocean via the Panama Canal. Like a true citizen of the world, Shaw had quartered the globe as few writers of his time had done (or had the means to do). But what value his travels had for him is open to question. It was Charlotte who, initially at least, made him into a traveller. The journeys he himself seemed most to relish were the early, adventurous motor trips, venturing at the wheel with a verve worthy of Mr Toad, along dusty, pot-holed tracks in North Africa, scrabbling up gravel roads in the Alps, lurching across Irish bog-lands. Sea cruises, though they afforded leisure to write, cut him off from his secretary, from his mail, separated him from what was going on in his own world of the theatre and of the many societies which had his patronage. He could not take long walks, or bicycle rides, or saw logs. Despite being the most famous passenger, Shaw did not

sit at the Captain's table on board ship, and exercise his cor-
uscating wit on other VIPs. He and Charlotte normally had a
table together in a corner, and ate as they invariably did, each
with a book in front of them. Interviewed when his cruise
ship docked at Colombo, he said about travelling: 'It is the
most unpleasant thing in the world.' Shaw used his travels to
spread both his own doctrines and his own fame, through
lectures, speeches and interviews. But his own inspirations
and ideas came far more from his reading – the New Zea-
landers noted with some awe that he had read twenty-two
books on the voyage out – and conversations with his closest
friends and associates, than from his journeyings. Although
some of his later plays, like 'The Simpleton', are garnished
with scenery observed on his travels, Shaw was not greatly
interested in landscape for its own sake. The English writer J.
B. Priestley, who met him at the Grand Canyon, heard Shaw
mutter something about its not being different to Cheddar
Gorge in England; to St John Ervine, on a country drive in
Devon, he said all trees looked the same to him. But in an
1896 interview he had remarked on the beauty of the sky
over Dalkey when he was a boy, and said: 'I always look at
the sky'.

During this last cruise Shaw began to write a play about
international power politics, 'Geneva'. The Swiss city was the
headquarters of the League of Nations, the pre-war forerunner of the United Nations. Shaw had seen the League in action in 1928, and had written a Fabian pamphlet about it. At
that time he believed firmly in its aims; by 1938 it was still
possible to believe in its aims, but far more difficult to believe that the League had the slightest chance of affecting the

renewed movement towards a European war. The play brings the three most celebrated dictators of Europe, Hitler ('Battler'), Mussolini ('Bombardone'), and Franco ('Flanco'), to justify themselves before the League's International Court. 'Geneva' is an anti-war play written when war was already being actively planned; its world premiere, ironically, was in July 1938 in Warsaw, the first city to be shattered in World War Two, and it was a popular success when it opened a month later in Malvern, transferring to London in November. When war was finally declared, Shaw built this into the play and wrote to the producer saying: 'The declaration of war is the making of 'Geneva', which has always lacked a substantial climax.' He had many other views on the war and it would be a total travesty to suggest he welcomed it in order to round off one of his plays effectively. But the remark points again to the insensitivity of Shaw to events which he saw as inevitable, or part of an ultra-human process; this somehow drained their human-ness for him, despite the fact they might destroy millions of lives. Another aspect of this insensitivity made 'Geneva' an unacceptable play to many of his American Jewish colleagues, including Lawrence Langner. The New York Theatre Guild refused it, and Langner pleaded with Shaw to alter the ineffectual and demeaning role of the Jewish spokesman in the play. Shaw was under no illusions about the desperate plight of the Jews, and was not anti-semitist. But he had not conceived the play as a defence of the Jews, or as an indictment of Hitler for his treatment of them. Events soon left 'Geneva' far behind, and Shaw was content to leave it there; even at the end of 1938 he himself called it 'a horrible play'.

He began on a new play almost immediately, an amiable re-creation of the court life of Charles II, 'In Good King Charles's Golden Days'. Far removed from the travails of 1939, it presented a confident portrait of England when that country was leading the world in intellectual life, and was vigorously creative too in the arts. In fact, Shaw specifically joins these two strands into a single one; referring to the artist Kneller and the scientist Newton, the Duchesse de Kérouaille (Charles's mistress and not previously renowned for her intellectual discourse) says that they: 'seem to mean exactly the same thing; only one calls it beauty and the other gravitation.' The play, his fiftieth, and expected by most to be his last, was well received and had a very successful run.

One of the Shavian shibboleths, as far as the general public was concerned, was his health. He had always made rather a thing of his health, as a compliment to his own life-style. After all, he was venerably old, and still active in mind and body. Surely part of the credit should go to woollen underwear, knickerbocker suits, and a vegetarian, alcohol-free diet, as well as to hardy generations of Shaw and Gurly ancestors? In fact, in 1938 and 1939, he was far from well. Early in 1939 he collapsed, in a state of extreme weakness, and was diagnosed as suffering from pernicious anaemia. The treatment prescribed was liver-extract injections, to build up the red corpuscles in his bloodstream. He was most reluctant about this, both on vegetarian grounds and because he had long been a vehement opponent of experiments on animals (he was well-aware that such research had contributed to the treatment he was now receiving). But under pressure from Charlotte, who herself suffered from bronchial and arthritic problems, he agreed. Soon the news got out that the sage of vegetarianism was being fed on meat, a story which he quite properly refuted. He was soon able to change the treatment to an extract of yeast. But he was becoming very thin, and, in a letter which reminds the reader of his sister Lucy's death from virtual self-starvation, he wrote to Henry Salt: 'My most distressing complaint is Anorexia, or dislike of food'. He needed frequent rest and sleep. Part of what kept him going was his sense of responsibility for Charlotte, who had aged considerably, and who, as a lifelong pacifist, was more upset than he about the advent of another world war.

In the early stages of the war, Shaw was optimistic, believing, as many others did too, that it would soon be over. In the early period of the 'phoney war' he argued for a Peace Conference to settle matters. His view had changed since 1914 and *Common Sense About the War;* he thought this time Britain had been pushed prematurely into war, and for the wrong reason. Common sense told him that it was unrealistic of Britain to attempt the defence of Poland, and felt that with the occupation of Poland, the state of war should end. But the war had scarcely begun. In two years, Ayot St Lawrence, not far beyond the northern edges of London, would see and hear the blitzing of London, and the occasional bomb would fall even among its orchards and gardens.

In Shaw's native country, by now effectively an independent state, the Second World War was something that was happening elsewhere. In Ireland, the time was called 'the Emergency' and the country was forced to adapt to the conditions caused by disruption of trade and the fact that one of the belligerent powers possessed the sovereignty of six nothern counties and was waging war vigorously from there. On one celebrated occasion Dublin sent its fire engines to help put out the fires raging in heavily bombed Belfast. But the atmosphere between London and Dublin was chilly in the extreme. Shaw accepted the British government view that de Valera's government should have allowed Britain to occupy its former Irish naval bases for the duration of the war. His opinions about the war were mostly unfashionable; he still saw himself as the Irishman, sympathetic but detached. Loyal to his view of Stalin, he urged the government to be placatory towards Moscow, before the Nazi-Soviet pact. Horrified by the effects of mass bombing, he did not pretend to the insouciance he had shown about the destruction 'for their benefit' of old French towns in 1917, and campaigned for an international agreement to stop the tit-for-tat bombing of civilian centres. He prepared one broadcast for the BBC, which was banned, and thereafter most of his wartime journalism appeared in the Scottish left-wing paper *Forward,* though he also wrote many letters to the broadsheets.

In the winter of 1939–40, worry about the war and the stress of looking after Shaw caused Charlotte to have a nervous breakdown, and from then on she was in steady decline. Not until 1942 was her condition diagnosed as osteitis deformans, a progressively crippling bone disease that was bending her double. Shaw wrote to St John Ervine that it was incurable: 'I was vetted lately and pronounced sound, but that means only that when I go I shall go all at once. We are both deaf; and the number of familiar names that we cannot remember increases ... I can still write a bit; but that is all . . .' Charlotte died, at eighty-six, on September 12, 1943. Beatrice Webb had died in April of that year. Their two aged husbands lived on. Shaw was deeply moved by Charlotte's last days, in which the stress of age and illness left her with the face of the young girl she once had been.

'Mr Bernard Shaw has received such a prodigious mass of letters on the occasion of his wife's death that, though he has read and values them all, any attempt to acknowledge them individually is beyond his powers. He therefore begs his friends and hers to be content with this omnibus reply, and he assures them that a very happy ending to a very long life has left him awaiting his own in perfect serenity.'

– this personal notice was inserted in *The Times* after the secular cremation ceremony at Golders Green.

Although Shaw the journalist and commentator had been sidelined, Shaw the dramatist enjoyed a brilliant wartime career. Revival after revival was staged triumphantly in London and other provincial cities. A new generation of stars, like Vivien Leigh, Laurence Olivier and Deborah Kerr, remade his great roles for themselves. The earnings from his plays were so great that Shaw was paying most of the money to the government under the wartime tax laws. 'Another "success" would ruin me', he said. The flood of new productions more than compensated for the lack of income from Germany and Austria, where he had been, well into the Nazi years, one of the most popular playwrights. Times were harder for his German-language translator, Siegfried Trebitsch, no longer young and idealistic, but a weary, anxious refugee with a reduced income. But Shaw was generous to him, as he was to many others.

In part simply to keep himself occupied in the only way he knew how, by writing, Shaw spent much time working on what he saw as a new political textbook, *Everybody's Political What's What.* This was published in 1944. Shaw's aim was to set out the elementary guidelines for the citizens of the modern state, to enable them to undertake their civic duties with understanding and responsibility. It was a great success, selling more than 85,000 copies in its first year. Shaw the teacher had scored his final triumph with his large class. The war had brought about a strong demand for education and a vigorous response from the government. For the first time, there was a sense that the future depended, not on a well-educated minority, but on a well-educated nation. Soldiers and civilians alike were not prepared to regard themselves as ciphers to be wiped off the page by a government eraser; the war was being fought for democracy and the value of the individual, so they were told: well, they wanted to learn what democracy meant, so that they could put it into practice.

Shaw's text caught this demand at its height. In fact, it was more accurately, as Michael Holroyd calls it, 'a political testament' than a textbook. Long and often rambling and repetitive, it looks back to the start of his political thinking and relates it to the era of atomic warfare. It was not an apologia; the old Shavian confidence might have worn thin in places but it was still there. He believed in his aims and in his methods:

'I am a Communist, but not in the sense in which it is generally misunderstood. I want to make man comfortable. He should have a reasonable remuneration for the shortest possible working hours. He should have more leisure for spiritual development and be educated for liberty.'

This last point was important. Shaw had no belief in the virtues of universal suffrage if they meant putting people like Ramsay MacDonald into power. He accepted that the Fabian Society had failed, making even less difference to political life than 'the conversion of the Roman Empire to Christianity by Constantine'. His faith was placed in human self-improvement, in collaboration with the progressive trend of the Life-Force, which:

'... proceeds by trial and error; and its errors are called the Problem of Evil. It is not omnipotent: indeed it has no direct powers at all, and can only act through its creations. Its creations are not omnipotent: they proceed by guesses; and evil arises when they guess wrong with the best intentions.'

Shaw's own logic and his efforts to maintain a magnanimous view of his fellow-creatures held him to the point that evil, in our present un-perfected state, was a necessity. Even in 1944, and certainly not after the hideous revelations of 1945, few of his readers would have regarded the Nazi government as a group of well-intentioned people who had guessed wrong. His belief in the inevitability, if also the transience, of evil, was a blind spot until the end:

'Governments have to persecute and tolerate simultaneously: they have to determine continually what and when to persecute and what and when to tolerate.'

– Shaw was, more than most people, aware of what an ugly mess governments had made of this process throughout human history. But he had optimism, indeed faith, in an educated future, in which evil would be a diminishing presence until:

'When democratic Socialism has achieved sufficiency of means, equality of opportunity, and national intermarriageability for everybody, with production kept in its natural order from necessities to luxuries, and the courts of justice unembarrassed by mercenary barristers, its work will be done'.

In army education classes, ill-lit air-raid shelters, branches of the Workers' Education Association, and thousands of homes, a great 'Amen' might be breathed to that. Shaw-the-Teacher was not the least important agent in bringing about the enormous Labour victory in Great Britain's first post-war general election (though it produced a government of which he deeply disapproved).

CHAPTER XII

*T*HE LAST YEARS

Since the shock of 1934's heart attack, at least, the editors of obituary columns had had their entries on Shaw ready. But they had to keep on updating them. Who would have thought the old man had so many years in him? A profile in the *Observer*, in July 1946, saluting his ninetieth birthday, acknowledged his own feeling that though physically he was failing, 'my mind still feels capable of growth, for my curiosity is keener than ever. My soul goes marching on: and, if the Life Force would give me a body as durable as my mind ... I might begin a political career as a junior civil servant and evolve into a capable Cabinet Minister in another hundred years or so.' The quotation was from a new postscript written for 'Back to Methuselah'. A reporter interviewing him on his ninetieth birthday said he hoped he would be able to do so again on his hundredth. 'I don't see why not,' rejoined Shaw, 'you look healthy enough to me.'

Since the death of Charlotte, he had felt dreadfully alone. Her death did not spark the guilt that Emma Hardy's did in her husband Thomas, or Jane Carlyle's in her husband Thomas. He had neither ignored not exploited her, and she had died serenely after a long companionship. There were even moments when he could feel liberated. He resumed his correspondence with Molly Tompkins, now back in the United States: 'We can write more freely now that Charlotte can never read our letters'. But he was horrified when his overture resulted in a proposal that Molly should come across the Atlantic for a last adventure. It would be a scandal in the village, a degradation to Literature, an insult to Charlotte's memory: he would be justified in shooting her if she turned up at his gate. He was protected by a redoubtable housekeeper, Mrs Laden, and his secretary of many years, Miss Patch. With Lady Astor, who had appointed herself as a sort of external guardian, they made a formidable trio. Mrs Laden made him eat his meals, Miss Patch maintained his lines of contact with a demanding outside world, and Lady Astor made him laugh. He had outlived almost all his friends. Sidney Webb lived on until 1947, disabled by a stroke, but although they continued to correspond affectionately, they were no longer able to meet.

At the end of the war, Shaw offered the unfashionable opinion that the surviving leaders of the defeated countries should not be prosecuted. His vision of them, slinking through the streets, discredited and forgotten, seemed to him to be punishment enough. He remembered the ugly triumphalism of 1919 and how the Treaty of Versailles had merely set the terms on which the next great war would be fought, and feared that the same mistake was being made by the victorious Allies. Nor did he believe in the separation of guilt. In the blanket-bombing of German cities and the atom-bombing of Hiroshima and Nagasaki, he saw crimes as great as any committed by the Germans and Japanese.

In 1946 he wrote his last complete play, 'Buoyant Billions'. As with many of his plays, its idea had been in his mind for a long time; he had begun it in 1936, then dropped it for ten years. Anticipating criticisms of its undramatic structure, he wrote: 'As long as I live I must write. If I stopped writing I should die for want of something to do.' The play is a romance, dedicated to the peaceful use of technology and the mutual acceptance of differences of creed. In a somewhat poignant passage, a character remarks:

'... there is one experience no woman has ever regretted, and that experience is motherhood. Celibacy for a woman is *il gran rifiuto,* the great refusal of her destiny, of the purpose of life which comes before all personal considerations: the replacement of the dead by the living.'

– this was something that he and his wife had failed to accomplish; and these were lines that would never have been written in Charlotte Shaw's lifetime.

Other short works were still to follow, a set of *Farfetched Fables,* a puppet play, *Shakes versus Shaw,* an autobiographical set of *Sixteen Self-Sketches,* the scenario of a new play, 'Why She Would Not'. By now an international Shaw industry was under way. The stream of theatrical productions all over the world went on, with Germany once again participating. A torrent of business and personal correspondence poured in from all these countries, with a new note being added by the queries of research students. Shaw's plays had been added to 'English Literature'. The three guardian ladies were troubled by the intrusion of predatory males into the domain where they cared for their illustrious charge. A local neighbour, Stephen Winsten, became proprietorial, and wrote *Days With Bernard Shaw*. A Scottish literary hack, John Wardrop, turned himself into an amanuensis on *Everybody's Political What's What*. A Jewish refugee from Germany, Dr Fritz Loewenstein, appointed himself as Shaw's bibliographer and alarmed Shaw by creating a Shaw Society: 'I only hope no-one will join it, and that there will be no proceedings'. All three felt it was only right that Shaw should maintain them financially, and a complex web of rivalry and mutual jealousy existed among them and the three women. Wardrop and Winsten eventually disappeared from Shaw's life, but Loewenstein became a salaried secretary, defended by Shaw against Lady Astor's denunciations, which were fuelled by Mrs Laden's accounts of his snooping and eavesdropping about the house.

Within this web of care and contention, Shaw was placidly alone. He did not care greatly to be visited, though he received visitors kindly and cordially. His own company was sufficient, and there was genuine self-deprecation in the message to an actress who wanted to visit him: 'When one is still an elderly youth of seventy romance is still possible with Old Men's Darlings ... But for old skeletons of ninety they are unnatural, abhorrent, unbearable ...' He worked a little in his garden, sat outside, still retreated to his writing shed. The daily routine helped to sustain him, but he was steadily making preparations for his death. He had made and remade his will on numerous occasions, as potential beneficiaries died before him, and he made the final version when he was ninety-three. He had offered his house to the National Trust, and it was accepted, not as a building of any architectural interest, but as Shaw's house, and a great many of his possessions were left in order to show it furnished as he and Charlotte had lived in it. Other things, including many of the books from his London flat, were sold before his death. He accepted two civic honours, the freedom of the City of Dublin, where he had been born, thereby making his peace with a place for which he had more than once proclaimed his loathing; and that of the Borough of St Pancras, in London, which he had served as a vestryman. He knew that he could be buried with the great of Great Britain in Westminster Abbey, but he elected for his cremated ashes to be mingled with those of Charlotte's, still held at Golders Green Crematorium, and scattered in their garden at Ayot St Lawrence. In that garden, at the age of ninety-four, while pruning bushes, he fell, and broke his leg.

News of Shaw's removal to hospital brought the world's press rushing to Luton, to the amazement of the inhabitants. Medical examination showed he was also suffering from kidney and bladder disorders. At first a tractable patient, Shaw soon became discontented by the hospital regime and asked to be despatched home – weakened and ill, all he wanted to do now was to die. Hating being bedridden and absolutely dependent, he ate and drank virtually nothing. On November 1, 1950, he slipped into a coma. His last words were: 'I am going to die.' Twenty-four hours later, he was dead. The cause of death was given by his doctor as kidney failure.

As the news of his death echoed round the world, it called up an extraordinary wave of tribute and regret. Shaw had been a fixture in the lives of millions, and many of them felt as if an old personal friend had died. At his cremation there was no religious ceremony. The music was from his friend Elgar, who himself had died in 1934, 'We are the Music Makers' (an Englishman's setting of an Irishman's poem), and from Verdi's 'Requiem'. His friend Sir Sydney Cockerell read from *The Pilgrim's Progress,* a book Shaw had always admired; the passage ending '… and all the trumpets sounded for him on the other side.' Shaw however had reiterated his own view resolutely just a few days before his death: 'I believe in life everlasting; but not for the individual.'

He was known to be rich, and had no children or dependent relatives; not only that, the continuing royalties from his plays and books would bring in a large amount of money for many years to come. The publication of his will was awaited with unusual interest, and it did not disappoint those who thought it would be controversial, and were looking forward to a last Shavian gesture from beyond life's horizon. It contained irreproachable items like bequests to those who had served and looked after him, and to some elderly relations; and gave away many works of art to galleries and theatres. But for twenty-one years from his death, his earnings were to be devoted to the creation and promotion of a new phonetic alphabet for the English language, with at least forty letters (he had established that it contained forty distinct sounds). For the next twenty-nine years (at that time the duration of copyright following an author's death was fifty years) the residuary legatees were to be the National Gallery of Ireland in Dublin, and the Royal Academy of Dramatic Art, and the British Museum, both in London. The first and last of these bequests were tributes to places that had been havens and places of learning to him in his own early years; and he had been a member of the council of RADA for more than three decades. Shaw was convinced that common sense lay behind his alphabet scheme: it would ease the education of every child who had to master the absurd spelling of English; it would eventually save the government huge sums of money; it would help English to become the world language. He was desperately serious about it, and deliberately left a huge sum of money to 'kick-start' the process. But it was not to be. For the last time, the British public had its chuckle at the old arch-jester who had always wanted to teach it better ways. It shook its head at all that money going to waste on a madcap scheme, and placidly continued to pronounce 'ough' in six different ways.

Some Books by and About Shaw

Most Shaw plays are available in paperback editions from Penguin Books.

Eric Bentley, *Bernard Shaw*, Limelight Editions, London, 1986

St John Ervine, *Bernard Shaw: His Life, Work and Friends*, Constable, London, 1956

A. M. Gibbs (Editor), *Bernard Shaw: Interviews and Recollections*, Macmillan, London, 1990

Michael Holroyd, *Shaw*, Vintage Books, London, 1998

Christopher Innes (Editor), *The Cambridge Companion to Shaw*, Cambridge University Press, 1998

J. P. Smith (Editor) *Selected Correspondence of George Bernard Shaw*, Toronto University Press, 1995